PLAYBACK:
From Hickory Nuts
to Hall of Fame

by Elbert S. Jemison, Jr.

with Wendell Givens

$19.95

Contents

For Jess Ann,
with love and appreciation

Jess Ann Yarbrough as Huntsville High School cheerleader in 1942.

Foreword
WHY THIS BOOK

This account is not intended to be a formal autobiography as I do not consider myself worthy of that.

Instead, after much encouragement from friends, especially longtime close friend and renowned blind golfer Charley Boswell, I have sought to recall the fascinating people I have met, the interesting places I have been and the more memorable events of my 77 years.

Also, the inevitable birthdays and aches and pains that preclude playing golf at the level of earlier years all prompt a person to recall past winning times.

This book probably would not have been written had I not one day chanced to meet and chat with Wendell Givens, retired *Birmingham News* staffer, author of *Ninety-Nine Iron* (the story of the never-matched 1899 Sewanee football season) and brother-in-law of the late Charley Boswell. Wendell encouraged me to launch this project, primarily for present and future family members.

Converting a collection of clippings, photographs and memories into an illustrated account has been rewarding. I hope that friends and others who are interested in the game of golf and/or military reflections about World War II will find this account readable. But the original driving force was preparing it for my family.

Elbert S. Jemison, Jr.

Foreword
HE SAID, I SAID

For six decades Elbert Jemison has been living a double life in golf (he flinches at the "double life" description) as competitor and administrator. Because of the dual role, he has become one of Alabama's best known golfers.

When we talked, he questioned whether there was enough material for a book. How else, I asked, could he preserve his story for his family and interested others. He fretted about appearing boastful: an Elbert Jemison BOOK? And if we did it, would it be confined to golf?

Golf would be the focus, we agreed, but his boyhood, schooling, combat leadership in World War II, and the fascinating people he had met were well worth recording for his family, present and future.

A mutual friend had joshed that Elbert had never met a mike he didn't like. Yet, here was a person who had led the cadet corps and captained the football team at Sewanee Military Academy, who had served in combat in World War II and who had played with Nelson, Hogan, Palmer and Middlecoff, who had talked golf with a President at the White House, but who was antsy when I mentioned the word "autobiography." Sounds boastful, he said.

All right. Here's the Elbert Jemison story.

Wendell Givens

Acknowledgement

A COLLECTIVE THANK-YOU

Most of the photographs in this account are from my personal collection, which began about the time I started competitive golf. As the collection grew, my only thought was about scrapbooks one day. Hence I have no way of knowing who made many of the pictures.

Photo credit is included when it could be confirmed.

I extend a collective thank-you to newspapers and individual photographers, along with the many, many sports reporters with whom I have had pleasant relationships and who helped record much of what I have "played back" in this book.

So, thanks to the White House press staff, The Associated Press, *The Birmingham News* and *Age-Herald, Birmingham Post-Herald, The Anniston Star, The Gadsden Times, The Tuscaloosa News, The Mobile Press-Register, The Huntsville Times, The Selma Times-Journal, The Decatur Daily, Montgomery Advertiser* and *Alabama Journal, The Tri-Cities Daily, The Daily Mountain-Eagle, The Dothan Eagle, Over the Mountain Journal,* the University of Alabama's *Crimson-White* and *Corolla,* and the U.S. Signal Corps. For any I may have omitted, I apologize.

"Playback" of golf matches would have been impossible without sports reporters, broadcasters and photographers. I am indebted to many, among them: Bob Phillips, Frank McGowan, Benny Marshall, Alf Van Hoose, Jim Martin, Jimmy Bryan, Grantland Rice, II, Sam Adams, Mack Shoemaker, George Smith, Dudley "Waxo" Green, Rick Bragg, Ian Thompson, Bruce Bemis, Bones Long, Hank Collins, Cara Morrison, Al Burleson, Tom Self, Robert Adams, Cliff Byrd, Charlie Preston, Tom York, Maury Farrell, Lionel Baxter, John Forney and Doug Layton.

Also, I extend special thanks to Bill Legg, executive director of the Alabama Sports Hall of Fame and Museum, along with the many directors and inductees I have come to know during my long association with the hall.

Thanks, too, to my secretary, Mrs. Tura Sloan, for encouragement and assistance. And to Bill Meagher, general agent of MassMutual, and all other associates for tolerating Wendell Givens and me in the conference room working on this book.

Elbert Jemison, Jr.

3,000 see Hogan and Jemison win, 4-3 | Jemison Nips Rogers
Jemison aims at sweep ═══ | At Vestavia, 1 Up
Jemison State Golf Champ | Nelson, Jemison Defea
Jemison's **214** ═══════ | Smallman, Pascoe 1 U

Wins Highland
Jemison Is Low Medalist | Jemison Seeks Third | Jemison
In BCC Invitation Meet | Straight State Title | straigh
| shoots

Champion at work...Jemison brings in state golf crown | at **3rd**

viii

1
A Yen to Swing

When I was 7 or 8 years old I took one of Granddaddy Dillard's hickory-shaft golf clubs out into the yard of our Redmont Park home, piled up some hickory nuts and began hitting them here and there.

For those swings in the yard there were no imaginary fairways or greens or playing partners. But there was a real house with window panes, and in a careless moment, I sent a hickory nut zinging through a pane.

End of fun. I went inside to face the music. Dad got quickly to the point, which I translated as a suspended sentence. "Don't hit toward the house again," he said sternly. I didn't.

Did the hickory nuts help launch my golf career? Perhaps. Most boys feel the yen to play ball at an early age and I was no exception. But did golf start taking hold that day? And why golf? I might as easily have drifted into another sport.

Perhaps I began getting the bug for real when Granddaddy Dillard occasionally took me to nearby Highland Park golf course. After playing a few holes he would hand me a club and tell me to try it. I relished the chance to try my hand, although I'm sure I was very awkward.

Mother took golf more seriously than any Jemison before me, and although she didn't exactly set the woods on fire as a player, she liked the game enough that she encouraged me to play. Dad told me golf took too much time, but once I began playing in earnest, he became supportive.

I can vaguely remember, but with appreciation, being taken to Woodward Golf Club by first-cousin Martee Woodward Webb to play golf with her. Her father, Allen H. "Rick" Woodward, was Uncle Rick to me as he had married Aunt Annie H. Jemison. I probably was about 10 years old, which would have made Martee about 23. (We celebrated her 90th birthday in 1997.) About 20 years after those early trips to Woodward, I would return to compete in the Woodward Invitation Golf Tournaments.

WHILE THEY DIDN'T PASS ON a golf legacy, ancestors on both sides of my family demonstrated a love of country, community pride and civic responsibility. I feel pride in what they accomplished, but those accomplishments were theirs, not mine. I have always felt that I had to stand on my own feet, and that's how I have gone about life.

Permit me a family-tree capsule.

My paternal grandfather, Robert Jemison, Sr., was a Tuscaloosa businessman who married Eugenia Sorsby of Greene County and Tuscaloosa. They had seven children: Robert, Jr., John Snow, Annie Hill, Elizabeth Patrick, Sorsby, Elbert Sevier and Richard Wilmer.

Seeing a brighter future in bustling Birmingham, Robert Sr. moved to the new city and helped develop "dummy" streetcar lines, which eventually were consolidated with related companies into the Birmingham Railway, Light and Power Co. After he died, his children picked up the reins.

Dad was born in 1892 at the corner of 21st Street North and Sixth Avenue, went to Powell School, Birmingham High School (later named Central) and Virginia Military Institute. To say he loved VMI is understating. He always hoped I would follow him there. His career was in real estate; a side interest was waterways development.

Dad was an artillery captain in World War I years, but poor vision prevented his serving in Europe. He saw action in Mexico against bandit Pancho Villa. A fellow officer on that expedition was Lt. Col. George S. Patton, who would become my commanding general of the Third Army in Europe in World War II.

Dad, Elbert S. Jemison   *Mother, Dean D. Jemison*

Dad later worked with his brother Robert, Jr., in land development in such areas as Mountain Brook and Redmont Park. They also were responsible for several downtown buildings, including the original Tutwiler Hotel.

Mother, born Mary Hardeania Dillard in Florence, Ala., in 1895, met Dad when he was at VMI and she at Mary Baldwin College. They married in 1917. She loved playing golf and once competed in the Women's Southern Golf Association Tournament at Highland Park. But she was never a championship contender.

UNCLE BOB WAS THE NEWSIEST of the Jemison clan. Having been at Sewanee with Henry G. "Diddy" Seibels, captain there of the 1899 football team that won five games in six days, he established a real estate and insurance company with Seibels.

Newspaper files show that Robert Jemison, Jr., was instrumental in development of (in addition to aforementioned Mountain Brook and Redmont Park) Fairfield, Bush Hills, Central Park, Ensley Highlands, Forest Park and other communities. He retained famed golf architect Donald Ross to design the Birmingham and Mountain Brook Club courses.

Elbert Jemison, Jr. at age 2

Mason J. Dillard, Jr., Mother's only brother, was an ardent golfer who in later years would support my early golf efforts.

Elbert Sevier Jemison, Jr., arrived Oct. 27, 1920 at St. Vincent's Hospital, a few blocks from my parents' home on 28th Street South.

A quarter century later the post-World War II baby crop would be referred to as the baby boomers. Just after World War I, our area of Southside experienced its version of a mini-baby boom. Some of my fellow "boomers" would become life-long friends.

Not too far removed from the time of diapers, early golf-playing friends included Nim Long, Brooks Cotten and Sam Burr. Golf games in those early years helped me mold our friendships to be everlasting.

Others among my fellow boomers were:

• Bill Bowron, whose parents lived next door to mine. Two decades later Bill would be my fraternity brother at the University of Virginia. A chemical warfare corpsman in WWII, he ultimately became board chairman of Donovan Coffee Co.

• Lamar Ager, psychiatrist (retired), with whom I still play golf.

• Hugh Nabors, whom I knew from about age 10, rode bikes a lot with me and later was a golfing friend.

• Henry G. "Buzz" Seibels, Jr., whose dad was 1922 Alabama golf champ.

Buzz one day would be in my wedding and would remain a valued friend.

• Bob Ramsay, nephew of noted Birmingham industrialist Erksine Ramsay. Bob and I became friends at an early age.

• Twins Reese and Bill Murray, who became lifetime friends of mine. During World War II we had a reunion of sorts in a combat area in France when they shot a Frenchman's chicken to supplement our K-rations. In post-war years I reminded them that they neither plucked nor cleaned that chicken, but it was mighty tasty. After my visit with the Murrays, I left to return to my unit about 12 miles away. The Germans had attacked and closed off my return route. My Jeep driver and I had to take cover in a ditch to avoid artillery. While in the ditch, he grumbled, "Captain, that was a stupid decision to visit your Birmingham friends."

• Bob McCalley, one of my early friends (I was about 8) when my family moved to Redmont Park. He and I have had many fun golf games and lots of laughs.

• David Massey, another early-age friend. When, at about 17, I swam Choctawhatchee Bay at Fort Walton Beach, Fla., David accompanied me in his small, primitive, flat-bottom boat, powered by a model-T engine. I guess at that time I didn't know the danger of sharks. David became a fine dentist and I was his patient until he retired. Ladies proclaim David and my longtime close friend C.H. "Hop" Chichester to be Birmingham's smoothest dancers.

• Jim Grimmer, another valued friend of many years whom I first met at Fort Walton Beach. He became one of the most successful and prominent shopping center developers in the United States. In WWII he was an out-standing Army Air Corps major, who flew 58 combat missions and was awarded the Air Medal.

• Van Scott, an early golf partner. Van's family owned the Warrior River camp that was the destination of some of our bicycle trips. We were at the University of Virginia together. Van's golf interest faded as he became an out-standing pathologist. He died in 1996.

• Henry Badham, III, a fellow cyclist and still a valued friend. Henry's parents had a summer home on the mountain at Blount Springs near Birmingham. The home was the site of numerous high school-age summer parties as well as fishing and frog-gigging expeditions. Henry wanted to be an Army Air Corps pilot, but that was not to be. His pilot instructor caught him using his atomizer to relieve his asthma while he was flying.

• David Thurlow, a fellow pony rider in our below-10 years. The Mountain Brook Riding Academy was about where Mountain Brook Village is today. When my father went there to rent a horse, I would get to rent a pony. Because he came from the horse-drawn cannon of the VMI artillery and World War I, my father enjoyed the horses. David's sister Becky was the wife of my cousin, Al Woodward, son of Birmingham Barons baseball legend Rick Woodward.

• Hunter Copeland, outstanding World War II veteran of the Battle of the Bulge, who has done so much to combat alcohol and drug abuse.

• Henley Smith, another early and lasting friend, who became an excellent and respected surgeon. He also is a knowledgeable historian and frequent luncheon partner at the Redstone Club.

• Bew White, a fellow student at Virginia and fellow officer in World War II. He remains a very close friend.

• Jim Kidd, Jr., a close friend who has served with me on many civic committees. Also, a fellow Beaux Arts Krewe king.

• The more I keep reflecting on boyhood friends, the more wonderful friends come to mind, such as Bill Spencer, Caldwell Marks, Bob and Doug Shook, Irvin Kinney and so many others.

WHEN I TURNED 6 I could not attend grammar school at Lakeview because our home was just beyond the city limits. After three years of private school, my parents enrolled me at Birmingham University School, often mistaken for a military institution. True, many BUS faculty members were ex-military people who still had military titles, so we toed the line. I got an early taste of military discipline.

The BUS instructors used mental arithmetic to help us think fast. Even at that early age my self-confidence began taking hold. The instructors taught us the value of following instructions and of planning. Those lessons would stay with me, even in golf.

When I was 8, Werp came to live with me and stayed 15 years. Like most Airedales, Werp had a hard, wiry tan coat with black markings on his back. My parents had taken me to the Birmingham Humane Society to let me choose a dog and Werp, a puppy, was my choice. He cost $5 and came from an unknown background. But he came with a loyalty and warmth that only a boy and his dog understand.

Had it been one or two years later, 1929 or 1930, my Dad might not have had the $5 for Werp because the Depression would have arrived.

If I ever knew where Werp got his name, I've long since forgotten. He stuck close by my side – indeed, he slept at the foot of my bed until I left for military service.

Like Mary's little lamb, Werp followed me to school (Lakeview) and hung around outside until school let out. He followed when I went to play cow-pasture football on the lot now occupied by Compass Bank headquarters; he watched from the sidelines and growled every time he saw me knocked down.

When my buddies and I made bike trips, Werp often went along, but as he grew older he couldn't keep up and I had to make him stay home.

Werp would get old (15) and he died while I was overseas. My parents withheld the sad news until I came home. Recently Henley Smith and Reese Murray told me they remembered Werp. I think it could be said he had dog-celebrity status.

IN THE DEPRESSION YEARS of the early 1930s most fathers, mine included, stayed busy trying to keep bills paid, so they didn't have a lot of time to spend with their children. We had to find our own entertainment.

My buddies and I went to the movies on Saturday. We would ride our bikes to nearby Five Points South, park them outside the theater with no worry in those days about thieves, and pay a dime to see a western. Our favorite cowboy, mine anyway, was Ken Maynard. Parental influence may have triggered that; Maynard was a VMI man! With an extra nickel we could get three doughnuts or a soft drink. Spending-money was limited. I well remember using my 15-cents lunch money to buy black tape to stop a leak in a bicycle tire.

Occasionally our crowd would make a day of bike riding, going out Highway 78 west and on to the Warrior River, where a buddy's dad had a cabin. With peanut butter and crackers, cheese and other such delights, we would picnic on the river bank, splash and swim in the river that afternoon, then sleep on the ground that night.

Lying there under the moon with the soft lapping of the river and croaking frogs as background, we discussed such weighty subjects as playground rivals, cowboy idols, girls in general, and alternate routes home.

Another day we would settle for a shorter ride, perhaps to Lake Purdy. An especially rewarding bike trip was to Uncle Bob Jemison's Spring Lake Farm on Old Springville Road in northeast Jefferson County. It was a real farm with horses and cattle and two lakes. We usually spent the night in an old grist mill by one of the lakes.

Because Mother was from Florence, I got to know that Northwest Alabama area fairly well. Bob Ramsay went up there with us as we visited relatives. Bob and I found a great place to swim — in Shoal Creek, which empties into the Tennessee River. Improving my swim strokes there and at the Birmingham Country Club in later years earned me a one-summer job as lifeguard.

For sandlot fun we Southsiders played football, softball and kickball (our version of soccer) on the then-vacant lot (as I mentioned, Compass Bank is there now) where Alabama and Auburn had met in their first football game, 1892 I believe.

I mentioned earlier that because my Uncle (by marriage) Rick Woodward had built and still owned Rickwood Field, I got to go to Birmingham Barons games there. His son Al, two years older than I was, took me with him on highly prized visits to the Baron dugout. Yet baseball never became the magnet for me that it was for so many others. Football, yes; softball and kickball, yes; golf, like no other sport. But I was never more than lukewarm about baseball.

AFTER OUR NEIGHBORHOOD became part of Birmingham, I transferred from BUS to Lakeview School, where I made new friends and prepared to go on to Ramsay High School.

Just prior to entering Ramsay I spent parts of two summers at Camp DeSoto, at Mentone in DeKalb County. In those years DeSoto alternated as a summer camp for boys, then girls, and it was a great place to visit for four or six weeks — great scenery and all that. Among my fellow campers were Charlie Nice, later a Family Court judge, Bob Ramsay and Oscar Price, now deceased.

DeSoto had no golf course, but it did have a large, open field which served as a make-do after the grass was mowed. We got clubs and balls from home

With Hugh Nabors (right) whom I defeated for the Birmingham Country Club junior title.

and took to that field, hitting balls back and forth.

The camp director was Mr. J.C. Orr and that name will have a familiar ring to Lakeview alumni; at one point Mr. Orr was Lakeview principal.

Nowadays I relive adventures at DeSoto when I go there to pick up grandchildren.

Now, on to Ramsay. Bill "Cannonball" White, who later would coach at Howard College and Sewanee, was Ramsay football coach and the school had some big, talented players. I had anticipated playing for Coach White and the Rams, but that was not to be.

My favorite courses at Ramsay were ROTC and civics. With the military background in my family tree, I suppose I inherited a liking for the discipline required in ROTC. And I became absorbed with civics and history, so much so that one of my teachers, Miss Eddy, encouraged me to take speech. "You're already good at impromptu speaking," she said. "Speech class will add to your confidence."

She was right; my second year at Ramsay I was on the debate team. And I have been rewarded throughout life by Miss Eddy's suggestion and by the understanding and guidance of others at various crossroads in my life. You will meet the others as this account develops.

During my second year at Ramsay, I began spending a little more of my time at the Highland Park (now Boswell) golf course, as did some of my friends. Club assistant Ed Stacks stoked our interest in golf by lending us clubs, supplying used balls and suggesting how to improve our play. He is due much credit for my growing interest in golf in those early years.

High schools were not into golf much then, but at Ramsay we managed

to put together an informal team and play a few matches with other schools
— Anniston and Tuscaloosa I'm almost certain were among them. My long-
time friend Sam Burr recalled that our golf team was comprised of Brooks
Cotten, Jerry Goss, Burr, Edgar Stovall and Jemison.

MEANWHILE AT MY HOUSE talk began about my transferring to a
military prep school. In view of my father's service in World War I and his
having attended VMI, that was not surprising. With the encouragement of
Uncle Sorsby, who had served overseas in WWI, and my own enthusiasm
about Ramsay ROTC, the more I thought about going to a military school
the better I liked the idea.

Dad was a friend of William Hazzard, who had seen positive results from
his two sons, William, Jr., and Meredyth, having attended Sewanee Military
Academy. Meredyth's SMA class was 1937; he was cadet lieutenant colonel
and battalion commander, as I would be in 1940. Meredyth today is both an
excellent senior golfer and tennis player, having won the 75-and-older state
tennis championship in 1996. He was a decorated Army major in combat in
North Africa and Europe in World War II, having been awarded the Silver
Star and three Bronze stars.

Another strong influence was Ashby Marshall, a role model of long standing for me. Ashby, whose father was president of Woodward Iron, had played
cow-pasture football with me and had entered SMA the previous year. If
Ashby liked SMA, that was enough for me.

Indicative of the esteem in which Ashby was held: In 1990 SMA alumni
sent out a questionnaire in which was asked: What fellow cadet did you
admire the most? Ashby won.

At prep school decision time, my father told me, "I think it (military
school attendance) is the best thing for you. In light of what's happening in
Europe (the threat of war), you will need military training."

Once the decision was made, choosing a school was not difficult. Uncle
Bob Jemison and Uncle Sorsby were Sewanee (University of the South) grad-
uates. Uncle Sorsby had attended Sewanee Grammar School, a forerunner of
Sewanee Military Academy.

That pretty well settled things. But I confess another compelling reason I
wanted to transfer to SMA: I wanted to play football and my prospects of

An aspiring teen tees up.

being a starter at Ramsay weren't bright; too many big, talented athletes were in school. At a relatively small prep school I would have a better chance.

Mother wasn't keen about her only son knocking heads on the football field. My father accepted it as part of the agreement that I would go to a military school.

So, Sewanee Military Academy awaited me come fall.

Oh, I should mention that SMA listed golf on its athletic schedule. But with my lifestyle about to change, at that time whether I would play golf at SMA mattered little.

Meanwhile, I had company at home. A baby sister. Eugenia Susan Jemison (then and now called Jeanie) was born in 1935. Thus, she was 15 years younger than her big brother and only 2 when I went away to school. Despite the age difference, Jeanie one day would be my No. 1 golf fan.

2
Learning to Lead

A s I prepared in late summer 1937 for a major change in lifestyle — from live-at-home Ramsay High student to live-away-from-home military school barracks — I thought fleetingly about my golf aspirations.

I had won a couple of junior tournaments. At age 15 I won the Jefferson County Junior Golf Tournament, promoted by Ed Stacks of Highland Park. Four years later I won the Birmingham Country Club junior tournament, edging friend Hugh Nabors in the final.

With those two titles under my belt, I anticipated improving my game and entering more tournaments. But I knew that Sewanee Military Academy wasn't likely to set aside much time for golf, so what I expected was a demanding school year with no golf, followed by a summer back home with whatever golf I could work in. I was wrong, but not by much.

MY PARENTS drove me to Sewanee, a community comprised of the University of the South, Sewanee Military Academy, faculty homes and a few small businesses. The post-Civil War founders of the university itself apparently had had two objectives (among others) in mind: (1) unsurpassed scenery and (2) isolation that almost guaranteed uninterrupted study.

Those two objectives — scenery and isolation — applied equally to next-door Sewanee Military Academy. But SMA added its own distinctive element: a military lifestyle.

Towns like Monteagle, Cowan and Tracy City appear on the map to be conveniently near Sewanee and "big-city" Chattanooga is only 40 miles east. But for SMA cadets, those places may as well have been in the Swiss Alps; they did not figure into what SMA planned for its cadets.

Mother and Dad let me out of the car in front of Quintard barracks, said goodbye and left. That's how the military school wanted it.

Two second-year men were out front waiting for me. I would live on their floor and get my room assignment from them. They helped me take my few belongings upstairs, introduced me to my roommate, a congenial lad from Ohio, and they, too, left. I was "home" for what turned out to be three years.

At that moment I felt I was entering a strange life and I wondered: What do I do now, where do I go, what will SMA really be like? At least I knew why I was there.

As it would every morning until late spring, a bugle at 6:15 a.m. routed me from bed and in short order I assembled with other newcomers and upperclassmen outside the barracks.

In capsule detail: I adapted to barracks and classroom life surprisingly soon. Our quarters, although sparse, were clean and neat (they had to be!); the food, though far from home cooking, was adequate. And very quickly I developed camaraderie with other cadets.

I HAD RESOLVED TO SUCCEED at SMA; to follow orders, stay out of trouble, keep my grades up, advance if opportunity arose. In short, I wanted to be a good cadet. Not a goody-two-shoes, but a ready-willing-and-able cadet who could lead if called upon.

In the first few weeks of barracks life there are always roommate adjustments.

I met a nice guy named Ted Darragh of Little Rock. Because he was an upperclassman, we had to get special permission to be roommates.

Ted and I hit it off from the start and became friends for years. On returning to Arkansas he competed on the state level in golf; a few years ago we had him come to Birmingham for our legendary senior amateur tournament for 55s and over.

Other rewarding relationships developed among my golf contacts at SMA. Bob Destiche of Shreveport, La., for example. Bob was a 1940 classmate whom I saw most recently at a World War II veterans reunion at Sewanee.

After the war, about 1947 or '48, I had gone to Columbus, Ga., for the Southeastern Amateur Golf Championship. I stayed with Sonny Ellis, who had known Bob at Louisiana State. Ellis' mother told me her son had another friend, unnamed, coming in and wondered if I would be willing to share my bed with him. I would.

The friend came in after I had gone to sleep, and I didn't see him until next morning. It was Destiche.

I managed to make the championship flight, but a playoff was necessary to fill the last spot. Destiche was one of the competitors for that last spot, so I went out to watch the playoff. Here comes this dude in white shirt, red bow tie and yellow blazer. I confronted him with a friendly name, "Goon, are you going to play golf in that blazer?"

"Oh, sure," he laughed. He qualified, but neither of us won the title.

LIFE AT SMA was a prep school adaptation of survival of the fittest. Some newcomers learned in only a day or two that they simply didn't fit. Others stuck around up to a month before departing. All told, I guess we lost about one out of ten.

Why? For different reasons. The superintendent, Maj. Gen. (ret.) William R. Smith, was a former superintendent of West Point who patterned our daily routine from what some had been used to at home. We couldn't bring a car to school (I had a beat-up old Ford back home), we couldn't run out to the drug store at any hour, we couldn't visit girl friends when the mood struck, we couldn't go to the driving range and hit a bucket of balls.

Almost anyone will get a little homesick, especially the first few days, but after a while you get used to the routine, make new friends and develop pride in what you're doing.

I always went home at Christmas and again in the spring. I qualified academically for an extra weekend visit in the fall, but I was tied up with football. What I had hoped for before I enrolled came to pass: I played fulltime all three years, at tackle two years and at end one year.

My motivation in playing football wasn't to be a hero among SMA cadets, but I genuinely enjoyed playing. I loved the physical contact in both practice and games, and the camaraderie with teammates. And I must have demonstrated some ability because Dudley "Waxo" Green, a Nashville sportswriter, had some complimentary things to say about me in his stories. Waxo would come up and talk with me and other players after games. Years later Waxo and I would meet again in Nashville, where I entered qualifying for the U.S. Amateur championship.

SMA played some strong teams — like Central of Chattanooga, McCallie and Baylor — and some not-so-strong small-town schools. My first year, with Ashby Marshall as quarterback and team captain, we were undefeated, but in my last year, when I was team captain, we were something like five wins and four losses.

A standout memory of SMA football: Our coach, Major Peter J. Garland, scheduled a Friday night game in Chattanooga against McCallie School and another the next afternoon against Bridgeport (Ala.) High School. Needless to say, we were battered and bruised playing two games in less than 24 hours, so much so that the team was excused from reveille Sunday morning. But we were not excused from the regular battalion march to All Saints Chapel at the university for church service.

An athletic figure who later would become a favorite at Auburn, indeed in all Alabama, played a small role in another of my memorable moments at SMA. He was Joel Eaves, later to be one of Auburn's top basketball coaches.

At the time, Eaves was basketball coach at the University of the South and moonlighting as a high school football official. He was working one of my senior-year games when I, as captain, had to make a play-or-penalty choice. I was trying to decide when I heard a quiet voice from behind: "Take the play." It was Eaves.

Years later our paths crossed again when I was inducted into the Alabama Sports Hall of Fame and was greeted by Coach Eaves, already a member. He expressed his pleasure that I was joining the ranks of inductees.

DECADES AFTER MY SMA FOOTBALL, blind golf champion and good friend Charley Boswell would tell me that playing football at Ensley High School and Alabama had helped him become a better soldier. I experienced the same benefit from SMA football.

As any player would, I got a real kick out of catching a rare touchdown pass, but I also knew the reward of making a hard, clean tackle or a timely block.

My parents took somewhat different views of rough and tumble football; Dad approved, but Mother always seemed uneasy, especially after one especially rough game we played in rain and mud.

In my final season I suffered a severe leg injury for which the small Sewanee hospital suggested I get treatment in Birmingham, so I went home for that. After the injury healed, I returned to action, none the worse for wear.

I did fall behind a bit in classwork, especially in plane geometry. But I had high-level assistance in that subject. SMA superintendent William R. Smith called me to his office to help me catch up. Believe me, that's awesome, getting homework help from the Army's onetime second highest-ranking officer!

SMA football captain, 1939

My football play must have impressed a few people because Sewanee (the next-door University of the South) contacted me about playing there after I finished at SMA. I declined because for three seasons I had played almost every minute of every game; I wanted to be sure I stayed healthy so I could get my military commission, and I wanted to keep my hands healthy for future golf.

Surprisingly, I found opportunity to play golf during my second and third SMA years, and we had a school team. I set my sights on being No. 1 on the SMA team and held that ranking two seasons.

We had to arrange our few matches around military school priorities such as government inspections. And our inexperienced coaches didn't teach us a great deal. Not meaning to be unfair, I think we SMA golfers knew more about the game's fine points than they did. My teammates included Jimmy Green (his father had a Birmingham car dealership) and Toby Agricola of Gadsden.

My game, while far from great, was steadily improving, enough that I competed in the Southern Prep Golf Tournament at Chattanooga. Tournament chairman was A. Pollock "Polly" Boyd, a friend of Bobby Jones and a great leader of young men. In 1951 when I was elected to the board of directors of the Southern Golf Association, Polly Boyd was a director and past president.

Tournament committeemen put us up in bunks at the Chattanooga Country Club and we players developed strong friendships. Another refreshing plus was getting away from military life for a few hours.

The Southern Prep event was a fishbowl event; college golf coaches could look us over closeup and decide about scholarship offers. I didn't win the tournament, but I played well enough that LSU and Miami contacted me with feeler offers, which I declined with thanks. I had other plans.

I saved my SMA days-of-glory recounting for last.

After two years at Ramsay and two at SMA, I had earned enough credits to enter college, but not quite enough to earn an SMA diploma or to complete military training for a commission.

My football teammates encouraged me to stay for a third year by electing me captain for the 1939 season. That honor helped me decide to stay another year. Then Superintendent Smith called me to his office and told me I was high on the list of those being considered for Battalion commander, every cadet's dream. Perhaps I was presumptuous, but I was fairly certain he was designating me the position. Incidentally, the other two leading candidates, Jelks Cabaniss and Temple Tutwiler, both also from Birmingham, were my designated company commanders.

School had been in session about three weeks in the fall of 1939 when the order was issued (that's how announcements were made): "Elbert S. Jemison, Jr., cadet lieutenant colonel, battalion commander." With that appointment came great responsibility and challenge: to be leader of the corps of cadets.

I had great admiration and respect for my SMA instructors in the classroom, on the athletic field, on the parade ground. If I had a problem, there was always someone I could count on.

For example, one day on the parade ground, I boo-booed by absentmindedly omitting a parade segment. The U.S. Army sergeant, Gilbert E. Naramor, a perfectionist, immediately called my hand. With a stern stare he demanded, "Know what you did wrong?" By then, I did and confessed the oversight. He could have demoted me, but he let me off with a reprimand: "Don't let that happen again."

I didn't. And I must have recalled his understanding years later in Europe. A sergeant under my command wrecked a Jeep, not in combat, and confessed the misdeed to me. It was a rare mistake, so I told him, "I'll have the motor officer list that Jeep as lost in combat as it was one of several Jeeps in my command that already were in poor condition."

IN MY THREE YEARS AT SMA I had learned to live in close quarters with fellow cadets. The cadet corps was characterized by clean competition, not only for cadet officer positions but also for athletic recognition.

I was constantly challenged, right on through graduation day. The headmaster told me just prior to that big event that the graduation program as planned was just too short;

1939 and 1940 SMA golf captain.

he instructed me, as I was on the SMA debate team, to fill out the program by reciting Patrick Henry's famed liberty-or-death speech. Thanks in part to my Ramsay High debating experience, I managed to memorize and recite the

Cadet Lt. Col. Elbert S. Jemison, Jr., 1940, SMA battalion commander, with staff officers.

speech without a problem.

The graduation ceremony was in the chapel at the university's All Saints Chapel and it included a warm touch of home. The Rev. John Turner, rector of my home church, the Cathedral Church of the Advent in Birmingham, delivered the graduation sermon.

In addition to having been battalion commander and football captain, I received the coveted Sevier Award as the outstanding cadet of the class. The sabre I was presented by coincidence bore my middle name, Sevier. As I received it I remarked that when I looked at it I saw not my name but the names of every cadet in the corps because they had made the award possible.

I had been chairman of the Honor Council, vice president of the senior class and the member of the SMA debate team. But more important than achieving class honors, I had grown up, boy to man, at SMA. The highly competitive atmosphere, excellent instruction and close-quarters life with fellow cadets had helped me develop leadership and camaraderie that would carry over into an Army career fast approaching.

I was ready to move on. Europe already was embroiled in war and I wanted to be ready if called to serve, and first up was qualifying for a commission. Soon collegiate golf would come into play, but it would be short-lived because Pearl Harbor was not far down the road.

SMA POSTSCRIPT…

From 1868 to 1908 what was to become Sewanee Military Academy was known as Sewanee Grammar School. From 1908 to 1971 SMA graduated many cadets who went on to outstanding leadership roles in the military, business and other professions.

In 1971 trustees of the University of the South decided to abandon the military as the lifestyle of the school. It became Sewanee Academy. That was a sad day for former cadets of the Military Academy. We felt that our institution had been destroyed.

At memorial honoring SMA war dead with Meredyth Hazzard (left) and Wright Dixon.

Today the physical facilities, including our long-ago Quintard Barracks, now house the Theological School of the University.

From the contributions, totaling more than $25,000, of more than 200 former cadets, former faculty and friends, in April 1991 we unveiled a memorial in front of Quintard, not only to commemorate the site of Sewanee Military Academy but also to honor and memorialize 76 former cadets who had made the supreme sacrifice in American wars. Their names are listed on a bronze plaque emplaced on a large Sewanee stone, in perpetuity.

The 1991 memorial weekend brought together more than 130 former fellow cadets who had not seen each other in more than 50 years.

The Memorial Committee was comprised of Meredyth Hazzard '37, of Birmingham, Ala.; Wright T. Dixon, Jr., '39, Raleigh, N.C.; Dr. Digby Seymore '40, Knoxville, Tenn., and Elbert S. Jemison, Jr., '40, of Birmingham.

More than a half-century after attending SMA I still see the value of the academy's honor code and of being exposed to a regimented and disciplined way of life. They were important to my future.

Today St. Andrews-Sewanee School, which is the surviving prep school on the mountain, is non-military but it inherited important attributes from Sewanee Military Academy, such as a strong academic program, the honor code and an excellent athletic program, all embodied in a Christian atmosphere.

The school is in capable hands under Headmaster William S. Wade along with a most capable faculty.

3
At Virginia: An Ace
in the Snow

S izing up Elbert S. Jemison, Jr., wannabe competitive golfer, in early summer 1940: Generalities first. I was competitive; not obnoxiously so, but I hated to lose. I considered myself a well-rounded golfer, but one without special strengths. And from comments by associates, already I was being described as a player who could dig my way out of tight spots. I could create and improvise shots in troublesome situations.

Specifics now. I was not known for length off the tee, yet I was hitting what I considered moderately long, say 240. On the negative side, I had a tendency to wildness, partly because I was too flippy with my hands. Some of my instructors also had had flippy hands, but they knew how to handle that trait better than I did.

Growing up in Birmingham, I had made it a point to attend exhibitions when name golfers were playing, then at first opportunity I would mimic their swings. Sam Perry, for example, was a role model for me and for many other golfers and would-be golfers around Birmingham. Perry had won the Southern Amateur in 1929, 1935 and 1941 and had won the Alabama title four times.

The Southern Golf Association used to conduct driving championships with distance and accuracy determining the winner. In 1941 Perry saw me on the sidelines watching the event and prodded me to enter. I did enter, per-

23

formed well and won. Later that day he invited me to play nine holes with him, and despite his being 12 years older than I was, playing with Sam Perry was a thrill, believe me.

I benefitted from watching Perry's rhythmical swing. He was smooth in every move he made and genuinely courteous whether he won or lost.

But in 1940 I was playing more by instinct and by feel than I was through knowledge of the game. I realized that I would never be a top golfer until I overhauled my swing. I was good among my peers mostly because I didn't have many peers! Not very many people were playing golf in those days.

THAT 1940 SUMMER HELD little prospect of golf for me. I spent the first couple months in an Army training camp to further qualify for a commission. Much of the last month offered a respite as I prepared to leave for college, the University of Virginia, I hoped. I had applied there.

At Sewanee Military Academy, early on I had made known to the professor of military science and tactics, a U.S. Army captain in charge of training at SMA, a junior ROTC school, that my goal was a commission. He knew that I had all the prerequisites; I lacked only summer camp training, the 10-Series Officer Training Correspondence Course, passing a physical and reaching 21.

Actually it was quite unusual for me, graduate of a junior ROTC school, to make it into officer training. But the spreading war in Europe and the strong likelihood of America eventually becoming involved meant that this country needed officers and quickly. As I sized up the possibilities, I felt that only the age minimum would delay a commission — and the Japanese attack on Pearl Harbor, along with my 21st birthday, would erase that delay.

Normally I would have gone to an ROTC officer training camp, but because that camp was full I was assigned to a Civilian Military Training Corps facility at Camp (later Fort) McClellan, Ala., for summer training. Once settled in there I began the 10-Series Extension Course required of officer candidates who were not West Point or VMI graduates. Then my parade ground experience at SMA gave me an unexpected leg-up.

The battalion commander, a major recently called to active duty, was to conduct a parade exercise to demonstrate our level of march training for the post commander and government inspectors. Apparently his parade ground training was rusty because he had not been on active duty in some time.

Knowing that I had just come from Sewanee Military Academy and was trained in parade ground exercises, he had me assigned to his battalion staff hoping that I could "coach" him. We worked out an arrangement whereby I would march just behind him and would whisper upcoming commands so that he could call them out.

The arrangement worked out well for the major, the battalion and me, thanks to my recent training.

I WENT HOME after that camp hoping to find a letter from the University of Virginia saying I had been accepted for admission. But Virginia, a top university, wasn't the easiest to get into, and I was becoming a little anxious.

Mother had asked me to share the driving on a trip to Winchester, Va., so we drove by Charlottesville to check on my application. I saw the assistant dean of admissions who told me, "We are accepting you." Thus, I got the welcome news in person.

VMI had been revered ground to Dad; now here was his only son choosing Virginia over his beloved school. That probably hurt him deeply but, ever the gentleman, he didn't chastise me.

I had chosen Virginia for several reasons: (1) the officer's commission I wanted so badly was all but achieved without four years at VMI; (2) Virginia was a prestigious university; (3) it had an excellent commerce school, my choice of courses; (4) it had a strong golf program; (5) some of my golf associates already were there as was my longtime role model, Ashby Marshall, who had preceded me as battalion commander at SMA and with whom I had played SMA football. At Virginia, Ashby had bypassed golf to concentrate on boxing and football.

Student life at Virginia was a marked change from the regimentation at SMA. At the university that Thomas Jefferson founded we were very much on our own. A key strength I had brought from SMA was self-discipline. I knew how to apply my best efforts, I knew how to study and the wisdom of obeying the rules.

I was never on top academically, but I was determined to make as good grades as possible. That turned out to be back among the B students.

At Virginia I could not bring a car to school grounds and I had to prove I could maintain grades before being invited to join a fraternity. I enrolled in the commerce school, studied hard and was initiated into Sigma Alpha Epsilon fraternity, Dad's frat at VMI (by way of Washington & Lee).

My first months at Virginia were confining. In the student body of about 2,800, there were no coeds except for 16 graduate students. From September to Christmas holidays, some of us managed a semblance of social life by thumbing weekend rides to visit coeds at Sweetbriar College near Lynchburg.

The University was big on weekend social life. Much partying went on, limited largely by students' available funds. But during the week the social whirl gave way completely to academics. Keeping up your grades was a well-understood necessity.

FIRST YEAR AND UPPER-YEAR golfers played as a unit at Virginia, and that was a break for me. My level of golf was higher than for most guys my age and, frankly, better than most student golfers there.

To qualify for the Virginia golf team, I was told to play several rounds and turn in my scorecards to Coach Butch Slaughter. Apparently he was impressed sufficiently because later he told me that I was one of four players and an alternate who would comprise the team.

The No. 1 player that year was Dixon Brooke of Birmingham. Dixon went on to become the national intercollegiate champion that year. After the war, I enjoyed numerous rounds with Dixon.

My first year at Charlottesville I lived in a boarding house on the grounds (described that way instead of "campus"). My roommate was Vic Salvatore, son of a skilled sculptor. Vic played golf but, fortunately for me, he wasn't as good as he thought he was. So I acquired spending money playing him one on one. I let him beat me occasionally to keep him on a string.

We student golfers would go out to Farmington Country Club to play on their fine 18-hole private club course. We could go into the golf shop there but were not allowed into the clubhouse. Years later, as a member of the Executive Committee of the United States Golf Association, the governing body of American golf, I was given red-carpet treatment at Farmington.

One match as a Virginia golfer that I remember well occurred at Staunton, Va. We were playing either Navy or Washington & Lee, as I remember. A few coeds from nearby Mary Baldwin College, Mother's old school, had come over to watch the match.

While we teed up for a downhill par-3 hole, a heavy snowfall began. I hit what appeared to be a good shot, but because of the snow I couldn't see where it landed. I heard a coed squeal, "I think it went in the cup!" And sure enough it had, but I hadn't seen my first-ever ace because of the snow.

For the record, despite more than a half-century of golf, I've had only two other holes-in-one. I saw the second, but the third, in about 1968, was a shot into the sun on No. 15 at Mountain Brook Club.

Funny thing about aces: weekend golfers seem to sink a lot more than so-called uppercrust players. Maybe it's because they play more! Some of my friends have made eight or ten. My longtime close friend and fellow amateur before he turned professional, Paul Stapp, has at last count made at least 21 holes-in-one.

The most unusual ace I've seen was made at Birmingham Country Club by my late friend Arthur Crowder, who usually hit what we call banana balls. Arthur hit a par-3 tee shot that hit a tree, ricocheted against a vending machine, bounced onto the green and rolled into the cup!

Back to our Virginia team: We won about half our matches that season I was describing.

LOOKING BACK at my summers between school sessions, I remember after the first year at SMA I performed chores around home and played golf every chance. After my second SMA year I landed a lifeguard's job at Fort Walton Beach, Fla., and played golf at nearby Eglin Field.

Between SMA and Virginia, as recounted, most of my summer was spent at Camp McClellan fulfilling my summer camp training requirement for a commission as a second lieutenant, Infantry Reserve.

My second year at Virginia I lived in the SAE house, as did a student named Bill Dudley, and if you're a football fan, you will recall Dudley as the University of Virginia's first All-American, a truly talented back. I still keep in touch with him.

When the Japanese attacked Pearl Harbor, President Franklin D. Roosevelt stated to Congress and the nation via radio (remember, there was no TV!), that the attack on Sunday, Dec. 7, 1941 "is a day that will live in infamy."

On that December afternoon I was returning to the University from a weekend visit with relatives in Winchester, Va. Driving along the Blue Ridge

1941 Sigma Alpha Epsilon Fraternity at Virginia

Parkway I heard the news of the Pearl Harbor attack. At first I thought it was a make-believe show (like Orson Welles' drama about Martians landing). Then I stopped at a store and people there confirmed that the attack was real.

That day the direction of my life and the lives of millions of fellow Americans drastically changed. I was a 21-year-old Reserve 2nd Lt., Infantry, and I knew that soon I would receive orders for active duty.

The Army wasted no time. I was ordered to Camp Lee, Va., for the physical that would mean a commission. I had 10 days before being due at Camp Wheeler, Ga., but I asked and was granted a delay so I could finish out that quarter about the first of March.

Even though I was not able to complete two full years at the University of Virginia, wonderful memories and lasting friendships prevail. I had developed a closeness with many great guys there, including the aforementioned Bill Dudley, who was always great fun to be with.

A postscript to my golf participation at Virginia: I did not receive my letter V until 1996 at a University of Virginia gathering in Birmingham! I had not returned to the University after the war, so I had not received the letter.

Just as at Sewanee Military Academy, the honor code at Virginia was accepted and automatic, and is still protected and preserved.

Longtime friend Bob Ramsay had just finished Culver Academy; he, too, was granted a delay and wound up taking his physical at Camp Lee the same day I did. I returned to Charlottesville where I received a telegram addressed to 2nd Lt. Elbert S. Jemison, Jr. I was ordered to report to Camp Wheeler at Macon, Ga., March 15.

My college days, my golf, my summers at home, my life as a civilian were going into storage for an indefinite time. The U.S. Army owned me lock, stock and golf club. It may sound odd, but all that mattered to me was getting into uniform and starting the great adventure

4
Over Here Before
Over There

When I reported to Camp Wheeler at Macon, Ga., in March 1942, I was all business — Army business. This was what I had trained for and had anticipated a long time.

My first assignment as a second lieutenant was infantry training instructor. In 13 weeks we had to prepare recruits for combat, for kill or be killed! Was I prepared to prepare them? Frankly no, not without a lot of persistent studying at night to make certain I knew how to teach the next day, subjects such as mapreading, using the Browning automatic rifle, machine-gun and M-1 rifle.

As weeks passed and I became more proficient and confident, in my spare moments I thought again of golf. I missed it, so I looked around for opportunity. I found it through an old Sewanee buddy.

Alfred Sams of Macon was attending the next-door University of the South while I was at SMA; we met on the university course and enjoyed playing twosomes. In Macon I phoned Sams and learned he was leaving for service, but before he left he arranged for me to obtain a military membership at a Macon club, the Idle Hour, for $5 a month.

In late afternoons I went to the club and played nine holes, often alone. Later, on invitation from an acquaintance at the Capital City Club in Atlanta, I played there.

Sam Perry with Southern Amateur trophy (he won it three times). Meeting him on desert maneuvers was the last time I would see Sam.

AFTER SIX MONTHS at Wheeler I was promoted to first lieutenant. In February 1943 I was assigned to the 7th Armored Division at Camp Polk, La., and after a few weeks there was ordered to Southern California for desert warfare training.

The site had been selected by Gen. George S. Patton, Jr., in anticipation of Allied fighting against German forces in North African deserts.

Tank drivers were being taught to keep their vehicles at least 50 yards apart to lessen damage from an enemy bomb, but the drivers needed practice. So I was sent to a nearby Army air unit to request that fighter planes drop bags of flour at our tanks to simulate bombs.

Wearing coveralls and a steel helmet and bronzed by sun and sand, I drove 15 miles to a cluster of tents. I chose what appeared to be headquarters, introduced myself and asked to see the operations officer.

A sergeant pointed to the far side of the tent and said, "See the captain over there." The captain was facing to the side when I began identifying myself; when he turned toward me, we recognized each other. He was Sam Perry of Birmingham, Ala., and Southern golf fame. We celebrated old home week for a while.

After catching up on what little wartime golf news there was, we arranged to meet in Los Angeles to play golf. Perry said he had a buddy at Lakeside Club in LA who could get us in. We agreed to meet there in three weeks, arranged for the flour-bag air drop and said a fond farewell. I think I was the last Birmingham friend to see Sam alive, last at least in this country.

A week before our scheduled get-together in LA, I received a field-phone call from Perry. "I can't make it," he said. "We've been ordered to the Pacific." In late 1944 he was reported missing on a flight from New Guinea to Australia, then later "presumed dead."

The golf world, especially in Birmingham, had lost one of its finest. After the war William McWane, Birmingham industrialist, led a campaign to create the Sam Perry Memorial Trophy as a permanent trophy of the Alabama Golf Association. I was pleased to have my name enscribed thereon in 1957 and 1958 after my state championship wins. Belatedly, Sam Perry was inducted into the Alabama Sports Hall of Fame in 1986.

I did get to play golf a couple of times before the desert exercises were completed. Our regimental commander's family lived in Palm Springs and he had an unmarried daughter, so that worked out for me to go to Palm Springs a few times. As I recall, there was only one nine-hole course, O'Donnell.

STILL A FIRST LIEUTENANT, I was ordered to Fort Benning, Ga., in later summer and given command of a mechanized infantry company that guarded German prisoners of war in the Americus, Ga., area, as temporarily we had no tanks or half-tracks for continued armored warfare training.

I was on the verge of being promoted to captain when I was told to report to the division chief of staff, subject unknown. When I reported there next morning, I was told that Brig. Gen. Edmund B. Sebree, assistant division commander of the 35th Division at Camp Rucker, Ala., had invited me to contact him relative to joining him as aide.

For those who don't know, a general's aide is his alternate eyes and ears, his sounding board, someone who will suggest to him, for example, that he is being too severe or too lenient.

The colonel who had told me of Gen. Sebree's invitation said, "Lieutenant, you need to know this is the only job you can take or decline as you wish. It's a great opportunity but it's entirely your decision." I replied that I wanted to talk to my superior officer, Col. George Moloney.

I asked Col. Moloney if he knew Gen. Sebree. He replied yes, that Gen. Sebree had been at Guadalcanal in the Pacific theater (during heavy fighting with the Japanese) and was a fine person. The colonel reminded me that if I stayed at Benning, I probably would be a captain very soon, that if I became the general's aide, I would remain a lieutenant.

I phoned Gen. Sebree, wondering how he had heard of me. He was jovial and said, "Let's talk."

Then he told me, "Two of my aides were killed at Guadalcanal, and it's not my plan to have another aide in combat when we fight the Germans (which he anticipated). Also, I'm not the type of fellow to have an aide opening doors for me or holding my coat."

Then the general told me that he had met my parents when he was preparing to move his family to Birmingham; Dad had found a rental home for them. That explained how he knew about me; he said my parents had told him about my SMA years, playing football, being cadet colonel, and about my interest in the military.

Gen. Sebree had three daughters, no sons, and I sensed, I think, that an aide was a kind of substitute son. He said, "When we go into combat, I will reassign you to a unit within the division."

Finally he asked, "What do you think?" and I responded, "I accept." We had talked for half an hour.

So in October 1943 I transferred from the 7th Armored Division to the 35th Division at Camp Rucker to be Gen. Sebree's aide. Leaving the 7th was not easy, particularly because of Capt. Ben Freeman and Col. George H. Moloney, my regimental commander. (Ben was wounded Sept. 7, 1944 near

Gen. Edmund B. Sebree, for whom I was aide and later served as a combat commander.

Wallace Wade, ex-Alabama coach ; he was a lieutenant-colonel aboard the Queen Elizabeth with us enroute to Europe.

Metz, France. When he came home, he practiced law in Greenville, Ga., only recently slowing down. Col. Moloney, I later learned, was wounded in combat. To my regret, I lost contact with him, having transferred from his command).

To resume: In a few weeks we went to Tennessee for winter training and the weather was brutal. Our division move from Camp Rucker to Tennessee had us camp near Huntsville, Ala. I would never have guessed that I would marry there in 1949.

Gen. Sebree was a man's man and had a great sense of humor. He pitched his own tent and chose a hillside so that at night, he explained, he could conveniently answer a call of nature without getting out of the tent.

After Tennessee, we moved to Camp Butner, North Carolina. Knowing of my fondness for golf, Gen. Sebree suggested that I take time off to play in the North-South Open Golf Tournament at Pinehurst, N.C. Although the event was not PGA-sponsored, meaning some top pros would skip it, I wanted to enter for the learning experience.

Also, I was aware that noted golf architect Donald J. Ross, who had been retained by Uncle Bob Jemison and Dad to design the Birmingham Country Club and Mountain Brook courses, lived from October to May in Pinehurst. I phoned and asked if I might visit him. He invited me to his home and we had a most pleasant conversation in which he reminisced about his relationship with the Jemisons.

I would like to report that I played well among the pros and amateurs at Pinehurst, but "acceptably" probably would be a kind description. I can't even recall my scores. Bob Hamilton won the pro purse (of $750!) and Ed Furgol of Birmingham, Mich., was low amateur.

WITH TIME GROWING SHORT before I would be going overseas, I made a last visit to Birmingham and my family.

Perhaps my Grandmother Eugenia Jemison, the family matriarch, guessed this was my goodbye visit because she telephoned me at my parents' home.

"Come over to my house (in Glen Iris)," she said. "I want to tell you something about the Jemisons."

When I arrived, she expressed family pride that I had shown leadership in my years at Sewanee Military Academy as football captain and cadet corps leader. Then she got to her point.

"I just wanted to tell you about the Jemisons," she repeated her phone message. "No member of this family has every shirked his duty. If you don't come back (from the war), it will be because you did your duty and died for your country."

If Grandmother's words are viewed as flag-waving for country and perhaps for family, so be they. She had stated Jemison family philosophy, for her generation and for preceding ones: Determine what needs to be done and do it. In a modest way, I have tried to uphold that tradition.

WHEN I RETURNED TO CAMP BUTNER, on the spur of a moment I went to a nearby hardware store and looked at golf clubs. I chose an 8-iron, took it back to camp and stuck it in my bedroll. Fortunately, it was just the right length, not protuding beyond my bedroll.

No, I didn't think I would be playing golf in Europe, but I had a clear purpose for taking the club. I knew that if I made it through a war, I wanted to play golf. Having the club along meant a touch of home but, more important, by swinging the club occasionally I could keep my grip and swing in trim.

Acquiring that 8-iron had been almost an afterthought. But it was to cause an unexpected stir in the combat zone.

Soon after my return to Butner, our outfit left for Camp Kilmer, N.J., to prepare for embarkation to Europe aboard the liner Queen Elizabeth. All told, 14,000 of us went aboard the QE, including 2,000 Army nurses and Red Cross personnel. I was single, so that breakdown was of interest to me.

The ship captain advised Gen. Sebree that as senior officer aboard he would be troop commander. The general told me to help him find a deputy commander for the Atlantic crossing.

I reviewed the names of full colonels on board and noted that Lt. Col. Wallace Wade, ex-Alabama head coach, also was along. Protocol dictated that a full colonel be deputy commander, but Gen. Sebree made it clear he wanted-ed Wade "so we can talk football." He added that we would not be fighting Germans while crossing the Atlantic Ocean. He and Wade became warm friends.

After six days on a northerly route to avoid German subs we arrived in Glasgow, Scotland harbor for unloading. I have often wondered if any other soldier on the way to war had brought a golf club. Fat chance I would be using it.

5
Prelude to War

Scotland is hallowed ground for golfers; as most people probably know, that's where the game began centuries ago. But our 1944 trip to Europe was not for pleasure, and none of us leaving the troopship Queen Elizabeth needed reminding.

In Glasgow an advanced detachment (about 300 troops and 35 officers) of the 35th Division boarded an ancient train that would take us to Okehampton in Devon County, southwest England to arrange temporary quarters for the 35th. Some troops would be housed in hastily built wooden structures, others in tents. My assignment was to assist in fitting the 16,000 troops of our division into adequate quarters.

The lodgings bore little resemblance to New York's Waldorf-Astoria or Birmingham's Tutwiler Hotel, but we knew our stayover would be brief. We were on our way to war.

When assignments had been made for all units, the main force arrived and began intensified physical training to build stamina for what lay ahead.

Officers studied maps of France, focusing on Normandy. Troops went to the firing range to maintain proficiency, and all of us reviewed our training on use of gas masks. Gas was a genuine fear; if the Germans released it, without masks we wouldn't have a chance. Those who had studied World War I knew that Germany had used gas then.

In a few days Gen. Sebree was summoned to Lt. Gen. George S. Patton, Jr.'s headquarters in Peover Hall, a large mansion near Knutsford, England.

Maj. Bob Stiller, a Patton aide, advised us we would be there two days and two nights and would have our meals with Gen. Patton and his senior staff officers. As the lowest ranking officer present, I would sit at the opposite end of the table from Gen. Patton.

Gen. Sebree was there to be briefed on the overall plan for invasion of Fortress Europe and on when and where the 3rd Army was to be operational in Normandy.

As part of airtight security, before entering the room I was quizzed on several points, including whether I talked in my sleep, to which I responded no. That question may sound trivial now, but with the future of the Western world riding on the upcoming invasion, absolute secrecy was needed.

We were told the invasion would be launched between June 1 and 15, depending on the weather and on what our intelligence people could tell us about German troop positions.

At 23 I was the youngest and lowest in rank (1st lieutenant) to be briefed in the War Room. Believe me, for a 1st lieutenant to sit in on such high-level talks was awesome. Why was I there? Because if anything happened to Gen. Sebree, as his aide I would relate his information to Gen. Sebree's superior, Maj. Gen. Paul W. Baade, our division commander.

Anyone informed on World War II knows about Patton, the "Blood and Guts" general whose trademarks were aggressiveness and surprise. A VMI alumnus and a West Point graduate, he already had established his reputation against German forces in North Africa and Sicily. Now he was in England to help plan the invasion to win back Europe from Hitler.

During after-dinner small talk, I heard Gen. Sebree tell Gen. Patton about the 8-iron I had brought along in my bedroll. Apparently amused, Patton looked at me and remarked in his high-pitched voice, "By God, if you can kill Germans with it, use it!"

Gen. Sebree was a practical joker with a great sense of humor. While at Gen. Patton's headquarters, he asked me if I thought we should put scarebombs on Patton's Jeep. These were harmless devices that would "explode" when the vehicle's ignition was turned on. I understood his wish for a little comic relief but I advised against it. "No way," I told him. "They'd give you

38

a Section 8 (discharge for mental reasons)." I breathed easier when he agreed it probably wasn't a good idea.

On another occasion in England, after addressing his troops, Gen. Patton noticed the boots I was wearing. They seemed to strike his fancy because they were not Army-issue. He asked where I got them. I answered that the father of a young English woman I had met was a bootmaker and he had made the boots I was wearing.

A dramatic dresser, indeed a dramatic person, the general asked me to get him a similar pair and I was pleased to oblige.

(By the way, the pretty young woman bowled me over when I asked what her job was. Without hesitation, she said she was a rat-killer! England apparently had lots of rat-killers, people whose fulltime work was killing rats. Obviously the country was cursed with an overabundance.)

Back to Gen. Patton, whom I would encounter again during combat on the continent: The general, I would learn, was an actor, a motivator who was excited by war, and the excitement showed. Yet in his way he was warm-hearted. He plainly enjoyed killing the enemy, but was bothered noticeably by American casualties.

As books and movies have portrayed him, the man believed there was only one way to go: forward. He believed in surprise attack, that a good attack plan now was better than a superior attack plan later.

Gen. Patton was physically large, about 6-feet-2, weighed 190 pounds, and had a high-pitched voice. He personified the will to win and relished being around officers who enjoyed combat despite being fearful of it. To Patton, war was the ultimate participation for man; all else paled in comparison.

LOOKING AHEAD TO ENTERING the combat area, Gen. Sebree later told me, "We're going into a great lifestyle, although it's dangerous. We don't have to shine our boots or shave every day." Having already seen action on Guadalcanal in the Pacific, he knew the dark side of combat, too, and he would see it again in Europe.

Our last location in England was Tavistock with headquarters in a large manor house. I had found a large empty field where it was possible to hit a few golf balls, and I must say, although at first I had to hit alone, I felt a bit of

In 1995 C.B. "Chet" Hansen and I reminisced about our 1944 meeting in England when he was aide to Gen. Omar Bradley. Hansen's son Jeff is a staff writer for The Birmingham News.

elation when I got reasonably good results with the 8-iron. Later I had company when I went to that field, and I'll explain later.

As Gen. Sebree had told me back in the States that he would do, he now had me transferred from serving as his aide to being liaison officer in the division G-3 operations under Col. Walter J. Renfroe. Being in G-3 would keep me in division headquarters in Normandy and thus still around Gen. Sebree. In that capacity, at times I would be assigned to detached duty; for example, to an infantry regiment as needed, perhaps as liaison back to division headquarters to assure that one frontal line didn't outreach another.

Anyway, in G-3 I became good friends with Maj. Bill Gillis, a Texan I had known briefly at Camp Butner in North Carolina and now an assistant G-3 officer. He had captained the 1940 Army football team at West Point, so we had football and golf to talk about. When time permitted, Gillis joined me in hitting golf balls in the nearby field. With just the 8-iron and a handful of balls, naturally we had to take turns.

WHILE WE WERE IN TAVISTOCK and as part of the pre-invasion planning, Gen. Sebree took me along when he went to Gen. Omar Bradley's 1st Army headquarters in Bristol. The purpose was for Gen. Sebree to become familiar with how the 35th Division would fit into plans for the 1st Army. Gen. Bradley later would become an Army group commander, serving right under the supreme commander.

Gen. Bradley was widely viewed as a soldier's soldier, a calm, unpretentious, warm-hearted general who looked more like a school principal than a high-level military leader.

I sensed that officers and men under his command admired and respected him; in turn he seemed to care deeply about them. He was viewed as a fine military planner who developed excellent insight into German strategy.

While we were at Bradley headquarters, I met his chief aide, Maj. Chet Hansen, who offered me the opportunity to become junior aide to Bradley. Had I accepted, I probably would have been promoted very soon to captain and would have served at the highest level in warfare. But I had become close to Gen. Sebree and didn't want to leave him, so I declined the offer.

At one point during our visit, Gen. Bradley turned to me and said, "Elbert, let's go into the kitchen and see if we can find some chocolate ice cream." We found the ice cream and Gen. Bradley, the down-to-earth general, dipped his own. I was honored that he had addressed me on a first-name basis.

That visit was not the last contact I would have with Chet Hansen. Decades after the war a piece written by Chet Hansen and entitled "The Unforgettable Omar Bradley" appeared in the Reader's Digest. I presumed the author was the Chet Hansen I had met in England; a phone call to him confirmed that. He told me that his son Jeff lived in Homewood and was a staff writer for *The Birmingham News*. Jeff and I became acquainted and had some enjoyable conversations.

Chet Hansen had retired as a full colonel and was associated in an executive capacity with IBM. And, as readers would know, Gen. Bradley ultimately became chairman of the U.S. Joint Chiefs of Staff. He died in 1981.

Before leaving Tavistock for a marshaling point and embarkation from the English coast, our division was visited by the Allied supreme commander, Gen. Dwight D. Eisenhower, and his son John, a recent West Point graduate.

Gen. Eisenhower, who addressed each regiment in turn, complimented Gen. Sebree for his service in the Pacific Theater and told Sebree he was glad to have him in Europe.

My impression of Gen. Eisenhower, garnered in that brief closeup, then from afar, was that he was a good listener, methodical but firm in speech, a leader who radiated confidence and thus was a great motivator. Years later as U.S. President, he would add to the popularity of golf.

THE ALLIED EFFORT to retake Europe had begun with the massive invasion of D-Day, June 6. After a month of fierce, costly fighting, Allied

This time in civvies, 43 years later I revisited the war rooms where I picked up 35th Division orders. Churchill slept here during the bombing of London.

forces had driven the stubborn German forces back from the coast a few miles.

As our division prepared to move to embarkation ports at Southhampton and Plymouth on England's south coast, I was ordered to the Allied Expeditionary Force's War Room in London. The mission was of utmost importance; I would pick up orders for assembly of our division units at marshaling areas where vehicles would be waterproofed for entering Omaha Beach and for loading troops.

With an armed guard in the back seat, I rode in a Jeep beside the driver. Armed Jeeps were in front and behind our vehicle. The trip was made without incident, and I delivered the orders to Col. Maddrey A. Solomon, 35th division chief of staff.

Somehow, maps of France that were supposed to have been part of the orders package had been overlooked, so I was ordered back from the marshaling area to retrieve the maps. Returning, I almost missed the boat, literally, making it with about five minutes to spare. Actually, had I missed my LST's departure, I simply would have boarded another craft.

Thus, on that July 6 morning, a month after D-Day, we boarded the LST. Among others aboard for the 50-mile crossing were Gen. Sebree, Maj. Bill Gillis and our Jeep drivers.

The crossing would bear little resemblance to the June 6 invasion. Even so, no one presumed the Germans would roll out a welcome mat.

As we approached Omaha Beach on the French coast, German planes zoomed in and began strafing us. Welcome to war, they seemed to say.

6
War—With an 8-Iron in my Bedroll

In retrospect, the strafing we encountered as we approached Omaha Beach a month after D-Day was not a major episode. No one on our LST was wounded, and after landing we learned that apparently everyone in the landing force escaped.

But the attack by German planes was, for most of us, our first taste of hot war, and it definitely got our attention and increased our pulse rates.

Although he already had been under heavy fire in the Pacific, Gen. Sebree used the strafing to tell me what he obviously had prepared for just such an occasion. "If I don't get back," he said, "please check on my family and do what you can to make them comfortable. If you don't get back, I'll tell your family you were a hell of a fine officer and a loyal friend."

His words would stay with me through the war and long afterward.

In conversations back in England, Maj. Bill Gillis and I had agreed that we were getting into what we had long trained for, we wanted to get on with it and get it over with. Perhaps the military mind accepts the possibility of being killed more readily than the "civilian soldier" who had had only a few weeks to get ready for combat.

For me, being a participant in the war was the greatest and most honorable thing an American would have the privilege of doing. I knew that if we lost the war, we would all be eating German sauerkraut for a long time. And

In 1987, with Jess Ann this time, I revisited Omaha Beach where in 1944 our division landed after being strafed by German planes. Bloody fighting had occurred there a month earlier on D-Day.

instead of playing golf, I probably would be caddying for Germans!

Naturally I thought of my parents, my 9-year-old sister Jeanie, and of my dog Werp back home — would I ever see them again? I thought, too, of the people who had helped me train for this great mission.

As for my chances of going back home, I knew I was at risk, as was everyone else in uniform. Obviously the risk was greater for some — the infantry riflemen at the front, Marines assaulting an island — than for others. For those with wives and children back home (I was single), the concern about surviving multiplied.

After being exposed to combat, as I would be many times, I realized the truth of the oft-quoted line: There are no atheists in foxholes.

From talk among infantrymen as we trained, I think we figured our chances of being killed or wounded at about 50-50. Unexpected thoughts, too, can get into your head when the enemy is trying to kill you; for fleeting seconds I wondered: If I'm killed, will they put my 8-iron in the box with me?

AS WE WERE GOING ASHORE in Normandy, my thoughts returned to the here-and-now. After all the Germans were only a few miles inland.

Thanks to the superb efforts of the Allied forces that had invaded Europe on D-Day and already had forced the Germans a few miles inland, we were not involved in combat immediately. But even behind the lines, there were reminders of the enemy.

We had been ashore only a day or two when we saw a truck loaded with

This was a German defense position above Omaha Beach on D-Day, a month prior to our division's landing.

bodies go by. It was headed uphill and blood was dripping out the back. I said to myself, "Training is over. This is it."

One day artillery shells had driven us into foxholes and a shell that struck in my area blew so much dirt in on me that I couldn't breathe. I used my rifle barrel to push enough dirt away that I wouldn't suffocate.

Then there was "Bedcheck Charlie." Every dark night a single-engine German plane flew over our area, not to drop a bomb or strafe us, but to keep us awake! After several visits by "Bedcheck," some troops wanted to saturate the overhead with lead, hoping for a lucky hit in the darkness. But I convinced them they would be wasting their time and ammunition.

One factor that our invasion planners had underestimated was that of the Normandy hedgerows. Instead of our light tanks running over the hedgerows, the tanks often went belly-up, exposing them to German bazookas. That problem finally was remedied by attaching scrap metal to tank fronts; the scrap helped push the hedges aside.

By July 8 our 35th Division had moved between the 29th and 30th Divisions with the capture of St. Lo our first major objective.

At one point when I was in a combat area with Gen. Sebree (no longer his aide), he asked me to accompany him to see what had caused our unit to hold up. I guess he wanted to know how I would respond under fire.

We were walking down a wooded trail when Germans in a bell tower began firing in our direction. We hit the ground and returned the fire, Gen. Sebree with a pistol, I with a rifle. He had a map and called in artillery fire that quickly silenced the Germans. I hoped my response had earned his approval.

During combat it became clear that officers and men alike had great respect for Gen. Sebree's leadership and courage. He radiated the confidence so necessary in combat.

We completed capture of St. Lo on July 16. Then for a time we were stalemated and Operation Cobra, designed to effect a breakout, was planned. With air strikes and heavy artillery we penetrated deep into German lines.

BY AUG. 1 GEN. PATTON'S 3rd Army had become operational and our 35th Division was transferred from the 1st Army to Patton's 3rd. On Aug. 14 we launched an attack on Orleans, the Joan of Arc city, and by late the next day the Germans had cleared out.

Advancing eastward, by late August we had reached the Marne River, stopping at Joinville. Patton's 3rd Army had to wait for supplies, which were being diverted to the 1st, and that, we all knew, would ruffle Patton. On the positive side, we had a chance to bathe and to enjoy rare hot food.

Knowing Gen. Patton's orders of promotions and without my knowledge of promotion, Gen. Sebree acquired captain's bar insignia and presented them to me with a copy of the orders. I think my promotion meant as much to him as it did to me.

Another welcome break occurred in September when an American entertainment troupe, featuring Bing Crosby and Jerry Cologna, arrived in our area. I had been away on a mission and caught only the last part of the show.

Whether the Germans had gotten word of the show or were taking potluck, artillery shells were dropping fairly close during the entertainment. The show continued, but everybody was antsy. Fortunately no shell hit the immediate area.

After the show Crosby asked, "When do we eat?" Bing was a good golfer and I was fortunate to sit near him and talk golf. Among other topics, we talked about letters I had gotten from Horton Smith, who had won the first Masters Tournament in Augusta. Now in Special Services, Smith had written me, asking that I check out golf courses in Europe that could be used by U.S. occupation forces after the war.

I would meet Der Bingle again in 1972 at his Cypress Point Club in California, where we had coffee and talked about our wartime meeting. If readers need refreshing: Crosby was a good golfer; he qualified for both the U.S. and British Amateurs. His son Nathaniel later won the U.S. Amateur.

While on the subject of entertainment, I must mention Glenn Miller, the "Moonlight Serenade" man whose orchestra and music may have been our most familiar link with home. After Paris was liberated in August 1944, Miller's band went to the French capital and provided the GIs who could get there with a welcome touch of home.

I was among the fortunate. Having been in contact with the enemy 162 straight days, I was given two days rest-and-relaxation, time enough to visit Paris and hear the Glenn Miller band, my favorite music since Sewanee Military Academy days. Three of us, including our Jeep driver, went to Paris and enjoyed hot baths, hot food and memorable Miller music.

With much of the world, we were saddened when in December the single-engine plane Glenn was on vanished over the English Channel.

BACK TO THE WAR: Gen. Patton next formed Task Force Sebree, with Gen. Sebree in command, to liberate Nancy, France.

In turn, Gen. Sebree sent for me to help draw up plans for the attack. We met in an old underground fort that had been used in World War I.

We attacked at 6 a.m. on Sept. 14. Gen. Sebree and I were in the lead battalion throughout the assault, and the city was in our hands by next day.

On a late October day I was in 35th Division headquarters in a little town called Amance, east of Nancy, when a sergeant found me and told me to report to Gen. Sebree. When I got to him, the general, sitting on a cot, was in tears. He said simply and sadly, "Elbert, they got Bill Gillis today."

Gillis, my good friend and former Army football captain from Texas, had accompanied a forward observer trying to learn about German troop movements when he was hit by artillery shrapnel. Medics told Gen. Sebree that Gillis died instantly.

When Patton's 3rd Army ran out of supplies and had to halt, this place in Amance, France, was home for me and others on operations staffs.

I shared the general's grief. I had been on the scene when other soldiers were killed, but none were as close friends as Bill was. He and I had developed a special friendship. Our views about war and the need to serve our country were similar. Even our brief pleasure in hitting golf balls in England had added glue to our relationship. Hurting badly, I sat and mourned the loss, wondering again why good people have to die. But I knew that answer: War is no respecter of who lives and who dies.

Bill Gillis' death was a tremendous loss to the Army and to his country. He had been an inspirational leader.

As I remember, it was about this time that I received an interesting piece of mail from home. Forwarded by my father, it was a draft notice from the Birmingham draft board! I replied to the board that I was not in a position to respond to its notice, but if board members wanted to discuss it with me, I could be located in combat in Europe. I signed the response: Elbert S. Jemison, Jr., Captain, Infantry.

ONE DAY I WENT UP with an artillery officer, who also was a pilot, in an L4 single-engine two-seater with top speed about 70 miles per hour. My purpose was to help spot German troop positions that I would radio to our artillery.

I was very uncomfortable up there, but the job was part of my duty in liaison. We were shot at by enemy ground troops, but the pilot laughed at my nervousness. The risk was old hat to him.

We went into a defensive position for a week or two, then Gen. Patton itched to resume attacking. I got word from Gen. Sebree to meet him and other senior officers, including Gen. Baade, our division commander, in a Bioncourt schoolhouse at 2 in the afternoon.

We had been inside the schoolhouse only a few minutes when the Germans began shelling it. They apparently had learned of the meeting.

With Gen. Patton, discussing plans for attack on Nancy France, the next day, Sept. 15, 1944.

43 years later, I returned to this underground fort near Toul, where we planned the attack on the city of Nancy.

Seven soldiers, most of them Jeep drivers, were killed and others at the meeting wounded.

Among the wounded was Maj. E. Ray Taylor, who had lived in Rome, Ga., and now was Gen. Hugh Gaffey's aide. I was standing next to Taylor and noticed his breeches were bloody red in back. "Major, you've been hit in the rear end," I told him; he was taken to a field hospital. After the war I would play golf with Taylor in Rome and Atlanta; we had more than sand bunkers and fast greens to talk about then.

Gen. Sebree had suffered what appeared to be a minor wound and asked me to get him a bandaid. I suggested he should let a medic decide how to treat the wound, and he agreed.

Two corps commanders who had been in the schoolhouse consulted on their plans and decided they needed to regroup. When Patton heard of their decision, he told them, "Hell, no, you're not going to regroup, you're going to attack." That was typical Patton.

Playing back the war in Europe would not be complete without relating two encounters with Birmingham friends.

I had come to know Tom Gearhart, a first lieutenant assigned to duty in Birmingham in 1942. In combat he was a lieutenant-colonel and an outstanding infantry battalion commander with the 75th Division. During a campaign his battalion had suffered heavy losses and was about out of supplies. I was ordered to coordinate relief of his battalion with a fresh battalion.

Such relief took place at night. First I located the battalion commander and identified myself as Capt. Jemison, Justice 3 (my code). He responded "Col. Gearhart." It was Tom. He was awarded the Silver Star, among other awards. Had he remained in the Army, surely he would have been made a general. Tom returned to Birmingham and married Marion Shook.

On another occasion I was leading a convoy of trucks carrying about 250 infantry replacements. I reached a crossroads where a tank was blocking my advance. I got out of my Jeep and went to the sergeant tank driver to tell him to move. The driver was Clarence "Bugs" Moss, whom I had known for years.

AS I REMEMBER, along about that time Wes Gallagher, an Associated Press war correspondent, arrived in our area. He saw my bedroll with an 8-iron inside (someone may have shown it to him) and he asked a Jeep driver to tell him who had brought a golf club to war. The driver pointed me out and Gallagher asked me all about myself and the 8-iron. But he did not write about me for quite a while; he wanted to expand on his information. There'll be more on Gallagher later in this account.

One day as I was returning from a reconnaissance assignment, I approached a top sergeant and asked him what his unit was doing about a German patrol I had just observed over a nearby hill. He responded, "Sir, our company has lost its officers and we don't have a commander."

I knew what I had to do. "Well, now you have a commander," I said. "I'm taking over until we can get a replacement from headquarters." We routed the German patrol and I stayed with the unit several hours until a replacement arrived.

Near the end of November, only 75 to 100 miles from where we were fighting, Capt. Charles A. Boswell of Birmingham was badly wounded by shellfire and soon would learn that he was blind for life. When I heard about Boswell being wounded, I remembered him only as a late-1930s football and

This schoolhouse in Bioncourt, France, was shelled by the Germans, killing several American soldiers. I was there with other staff officers planning attack strategy. This picture shows the schoolhouse after it was restored.

baseball star at Alabama. In post-war years we would become the best of friends.

After the war I would learn of a coincidence about the Boswell wounding. A close friend of Charley's, C.E. "Red" Michaels, an artillery officer, told me he was in an L4 observation plane over the very area where Boswell had been badly wounded until two or three days after it occurred.

On Dec. 16 the Germans began a counterattack on an 80-mile front where Allied lines were weakest. Our division was not in the area; we were to the south. On Christmas Day we were in Metz, where we got a hot meal and a bath.

Christmas afternoon we were ordered to move out to help stop what had become known as the Bulge, the overall action as of the Battle of the Bulge. We attacked on the southern front and eventually with other Allied forces stopped and pushed the enemy back in casualty-heavy fighting.

AN INCIDENT THAT INVOLVED ME briefly with Gen. Patton, and could have changed my military future, occurred about Dec. 30, still during the Battle of the Bulge. It happened along a road from Arlon, Belgium to Bastogne, the main route north for troops and supplies to penetrate the southern part of the Bulge.

The encounter occurred one midnight when the temperature hovered around zero. I was on a mission to take medical supplies to a medical unit that had exhausted its original supply when our Jeep came upon stalled traffic. I walked ahead to see what was causing the holdup.

To my surprise I heard Gen. Patton's high-pitched voice as he expressed impatience with a commander whose unit wasn't advancing across a stream.

I identified myself to Gen. Patton, told him about my mission and asked about the stalled unit. He identified the unit and asked if I thought I could get it moving. Not knowing precisely what I would do, but, knowing the general's disdain of can't-do answers, I responded, "Yes, sir!" Gen. Patton told the unit commander if he didn't move across that stream, he had a captain who would relieve him. The unit commander then moved his unit forward and the episode ended. But it illustrates Patton's way of doing things.

Gen. Patton's military style was controversial, no question. He usually succeeded, no question. Count me among his admirers and thank goodness he was on our side. Since his death in a traffic accident in Germany soon after the war, I have read much about him. Perhaps the most memorable comment was made in a letter from one of his aides, Col. Dick Codman, to Mrs. Codman. It follows.

"I am quite ready to believe that there may be other E.T.O. commanders who equal our own in mere technical proficiency. I have seen or heard of none, however, who can even remotely compare with General Patton in respect to his uncanny gift for sweeping men into doing things which they do not believe they are capable of doing, which they do not really want to do, which, in fact, they would not do, unless directly exposed to the personality, the genius — call it what you will — of this unique soldier who not only knows his extraordinary job, but loves it . . . An entire army, from corps commander to rifleman, is galvanized into action by the dynamism of one man. Even his military superiors find themselves irresistibly, if reluctantly, drawn into his magnetic field . . ."

By late January all the territory lost to the Germans in the Battle of the Bulge had been regained, but the cost had been terrible: about 81,000 Allied casualties and about 120,000 German casualties.

Perhaps the following figures will help put the casualty figures in focus: An infantry division is comprised of about 14,000 troops (officers and men). During the war the two divisions I served in were the 35th Infantry and the 28th Infantry divisions. The 35th incurred 25,488 casualties (killed, wounded and missing). The 28th incurred 24,840 casualties.

That made the 35th's loss ratio 181 percent and the 28th's loss ratio 176 percent. The explanation for the ratios being more than 100 percent is replacements.

(Years after the war veterans of the Battle of the Bulge, all over America organized state chapters. I was one of seven organizers of the George S. Patton, Jr., Chapter. A few years ago we had 172 members, but as of 1997 due to attrition we had dropped to about 125. Our monthly meetings afford us opportunity for reminiscing about the Bulge, sharing our individual experiences. We enjoy the fellowship and we send flowers and sympathy messages to widows of members.)

AS DOES EVERY DIVISION, ours had a medical shock team comprised of a surgeon, two nurses and aides. Such a team served somewhat like a hospital emergency room, treating the badly wounded on the spot so they could be moved to a field hospital. For example, the team would remove shrapnel from a soldier who had been hit, then send him to the field hospital.

One day a nurse from our shock team wanted to see a little of what was going on the front lines, so when a firefight broke out, she asked me to take her where she might see fighting up close.

Bad idea. Foolish on my part to agree. But I did.

I told the nurse we would go to a vantage point that night, let her have a very brief look, then hurry back. I arranged for a Jeep to take us, also a foolish decision because I was putting the driver and the nurse at unnecessary risk.

Enemy artillery was firing in, using flares to focus the fire. We went close enough that we were at risk from rifle fire. The flares brightened the fight scene and quickly got the nurse's attention; she asked to get out of there pronto. We did.

IN FEBRUARY, Wes Gallagher, the Associated Press war correspondent who much earlier had noted the 8-iron in my bedroll, showed up again. Because American and British forces had linked up near Geldern, Germany, he arranged to talk golf with me and Lt. J.R.S. Wingate, a native Scot and British liaison officer.

Wingate talked about golf in Scotland, the game's birthplace, and noted that many of the nation's best courses had been plowed under to aid the war

Snapshot with Maj. George R. Allin, Jr., (left) at Nancy, France.

effort.

We talked about the best players in America and Britain, the Ryder and Walker Cup matches, and the possibility of golf during post-war occupation.

Gallagher's article, accompanied by a Wingate-Jemison photograph, was published widely, including in my hometown *Birmingham Age-Herald*. Gallagher's story noted that I was the only soldier in combat who carried a golf club.

ABOUT MARCH 1 GEN. SEBREE was assigned to the 28th Division as assistant division commander under Gen. Norman D. Cota, who had an outstanding invasion record with the 29th Division (Readers may recall that Robert Mitchum played Gen. Cota in the movie *The Longest Day*).

Before leaving the 35th Division, Gen. Sebree asked me if I wanted to go with him, presuming he could work it out. My answer was yes and soon I was transferred to the 28th Division to take command of the 28th Mechanized Cavalry Reconnaissance Troop with 280 men and 85 vehicles.

Gen. Sebree told me, "I may be getting you into a hell of a mess because this war isn't over, but I would like for you to have this command experience as it would be good on your record if you want to become Regular Army."

The downside of leaving the 35th Division was being separated from two very close friends whom I had been with since England: Maj. George R. Allin, Jr., assistant G-3 of the division, and Capt. Ernie Zielasko, who had been a fellow liaison officer. (After the war. I was best man in George Allin's

Showing my 8-iron to British Lt. J.R.S. Wingate near Wesels, Germany, March 1945. This photo accompanied Wes Gallagher's AP story that was published around the world. (Associated Press photo).

wedding. A retired colonel, he lives in Washington. Ernie Zielasko, a retired writer, lives in Florida.)

I TOLD GEN. SEBREE I had reservations about commanding the 28th Recon Troop, but he reassured me, "You will learn it in a hurry."

Every infantry division has a reconnaissance troop that seeks out and brings back information on enemy strength, terrain, roads, bridges, etc.

When I took command, a lot of thoughts ran through my head. It was awesome for me at age 24 to have my own command, something all military people relish. The atmosphere was strange; a cavalry officer usually commands a cavalry troop. So my first move was to learn the composition of the troop, its manpower, the four platoons, each headed by a lieutenant. And I set out to learn what those lieutenants had been through; their unit had had high casualties.

The headquarters platoon is responsible for the troop's food, supplies, medicines and motor pool vehicles. The other three are combat platoons, the eyes and ears of the division. My immediate superior was a lieutenant-colonel, the division intelligence officer in G-2.

I was replacing the troop's acting commander, Lt. Barney Skladany, a VMI man. Thinking he would be disappointed at not being given the command, I explained to Skladany that I had not sought the position but had been assigned to it. He wasn't disappointed, he was relieved, he said. He didn't want to be commander, preferring to be executive officer.

Barney and I got along splendidly and within a few days I felt comfortable with the officers and troops. I formed a special friendship with Lt. Dale W. Taylor, one of my officers. After the war, Dale stayed in the military and I recommended that he become Gen. Sebree's aide, which he did. He retired as a full colonel and went with a Savannah bank. We talked over our experiences recently when he came through Birmingham.

MY RECONNAISSANCE TROOP at times operated as a "total troop," seeking out information on the enemy and cleaning out pockets of Germans who had been bypassed and fought much like vigilantes. At other times one of our platoons would attach to another unit and take its orders from that unit.

We continued to suffer casualties, the worst of which resulted from our vehicles hitting land mines. One scene burned into my memory is the body of a soldier hanging in a tree after his vehicle hit a mine.

It was my duty as unit commander to write the next of kin of men killed in action, and that often was difficult, despite initial notification by the War Department. Writing usually at night, I tried to comfort each family, emphasizing that we could not win the war without the contribution of their soldier.

Before the war ended I had developed a warm camaraderie with my men, many of whom were older than I was. None seemed to resent me as their leader, and I tried to radiate the confidence that would, I hoped, persuade them that I knew what I was doing.

As the German armies continued their retreat, we sensed that the war would end soon, and it did end May 6, 11 months after D-Day. The first dramatic radio message to us was "Hold position and hold fire." The welcome "Cease fire" soon followed.

My troops and I had made it — lived through the war! Then followed the grim second thought: Many hadn't made it. And many others would go home crippled for life.

I contacted our lieutenants, who were spread over a 25-square mile area, and celebrations erupted. We overlooked all but the most boisterous and acted only to protect the few citizens on hand.

In mid-May I was ordered to move my troops to Kaiserlautern as the occupation began and the German people began returning to their homes. We got back to spit-and-polish, to shaving every day and generally trying to be clean and neat again. We were visited by congressmen, other government officials and various military leaders.

One of our duties had been to provide security for 1st Army headquarters. An aide there to Gen. William B. Kean was Capt. Bill Smith, whose sons Bill and Hatton now own Royal Cup Coffee, Co. of Birmingham.

After a couple of weeks in Kaiserlautern I was ordered to division headquarters to begin organizing a 3rd Army golf team that would play other Army teams. I was told to circulate through the area, locate prospects and to determine if they met my criteria.

Further instruction: Requisition vehicles and take the best 16 candidates to Belgian King Leopold's chateau. I had those 16 assemble at 3rd Army head-

My 28th Division Recon Troop (above) assembled in Kaiserlautern, Germany, during occupation in May 1945.

quarters, requested command cars and we were driven there. On the way I thought to myself: This is the reward of war — to ride up here like this and select a golf team!

By letting the team prospects play each other, I chose a team of eight that included Walter Burkemo of Detroit, a better golfer than I was; later he would be a PGA Tournament runnerup. Instead of sending those who didn't make the team back to their camps, we let them all stay and enjoy the luxuries of the chateau. We had great food and sumptuous living quarters.

Nine of the original 18 holes at the chateau were playable; the other nine had been plowed under so the Germans could plant potatoes.

Then, after all that preparation and without playing one match, we were told to disband. It was time to go home to the U.S.A.

Before leaving Europe, Gen. Sebree called me to meet with him. Several staff officers were present, along with Lt. Taylor, his aide. The purpose was to award me the Bronze Star for "Exceptional Meritorious Service." I was deeply grateful to Gen. Sebree.

Our outfit went to Reims, then to Le Havre to embark for Boston.

WE ARRIVED IN BOSTON HARBOR in late August and boarded troop trains for Camp Shelby, Miss. I told the troop commander that I wanted to get off in Birmingham, that my executive officer would take over. That

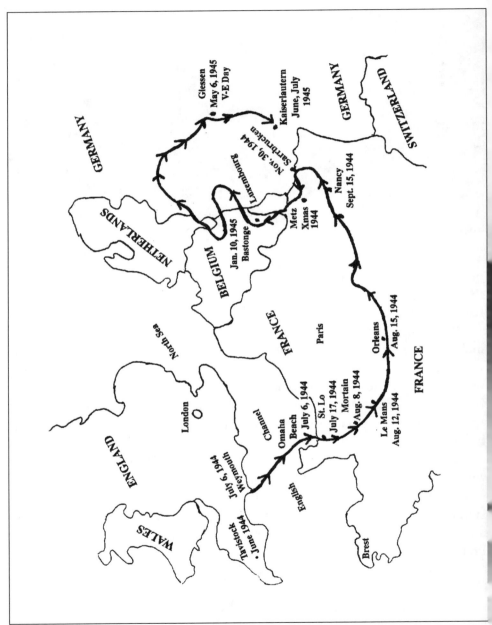

World War II combat route of Capt. Elbert S. Jemison, Jr., July 6, 1944 to May 6, 1945 (about 1,400 miles).

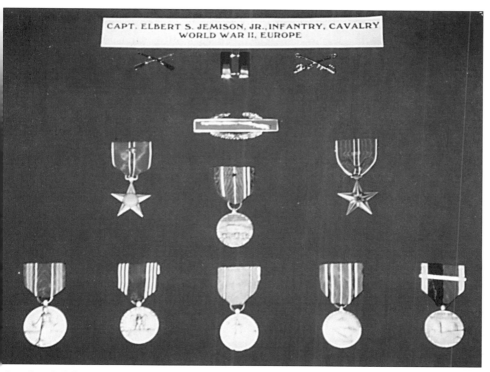

Awards included Combat Infantryman's Badge and two Bronze Stars.

approved, I got off at the old Terminal Station. Mother, Dad and kid sister Jeanie were there to welcome me in a grand family reunion indeed.

We stayed up late and talked and talked and talked. The only sad note was learning that my faithful dog Werp had died of old age; the family had withheld the news while I was in Europe.

I told them I had about decided not to become Regular Army. I had mixed feelings about that decision, based in part on the fact I was not West Point or VMI. Also I had had less than two years of college.

Still another factor: I had grown weary of being so far from home, starting with Sewanee Military Academy days. What finally tipped the scales with me, however, was a keen desire to get back into golf and see what the future held there.

The next day I drove to Camp Shelby to become a civilian again. Gen.

Sebree told me that he probably would be going to Australia as U.S. military attache; that if he did, I could go along as assistant attache with the rank of major. That was tempting, but it was too far from home.

As things turned out, Gen. Sebree did go to Australia, then later was assigned with Special Information Services, Army Ground Forces. He died in 1965 with the rank of major general.

In 1989 I wrote an account of my memorable association with Gen. Sebree, expressing my devotion and admiration for him, and presented it to his three daughters, Ibby, Marty and Toddy.

7
At Alabama: Classes and Chip Shots

S hifting gears from soldier to civilian had its obvious rewards, such as ample time to play golf, but the first few weeks of resuming civilian life were not easy for me. Over and over I reminded myself that I knew how to do only two things: Be an Army officer and play golf.

On the voyage home from Europe I had pondered: Do I really want to leave the military, give up a certain promotion to major and the chance to become assistant U.S. military attache to Gen. Sebree in Australia? I wrestled with the question a long time before deciding.

Nudging me toward civilian life were these factors: (1) I knew I should add to my less-than-two years of college; (2) after several years of living away — at Sewanee Military Academy, the University of Virginia and in the Army — I wanted to be closer to home; (3) I was drawn more and more to golf; military life would put severe restraints on playing.

For months I continued to second-guess leaving the military, but gradually I concluded I had made the right decision.

Now, what field did I want to enter and where best to resume college? Military life and my interest in golf stirred an interest in landscape architecture. I was aware of Uncle Bob Jemison's success in land development, and the military had taught me much about terrain. Why not consider a career in landscape architecture?

Auburn University seemed the logical place to study that subject, so I drove there to check on available courses. Landscape architecture isn't offered, the academic dean told me, and that was that. I returned home.

I had studied commerce for just under two years at Virginia before going overseas, and I knew that the University of Alabama had an excellent commerce (business) school. Also, U of A planned to restore golf to its athletic schedule after dropping it during the war. I had made up my mind on another point: If you live in Alabama, best to go to college in Alabama.

During the months before I would enroll at Alabama in December, I gradually acquired civilian clothes, re-established ties with old friends and played golf, mostly on the municipal courses at Highland Park (now Boswell) and Roebuck.

I went on inactive Army status in early October and accepted a Reserve commission as captain. By accepting, I would attend drill once a week in Birmingham, later in Tuscaloosa. And there would be two weeks of training in summer.

STUDENT LIFE AT ALABAMA wasn't all that different from that at the University of Virginia except for one thing. Two months before I enrolled at UA I had turned 26; that meant I was several years older than many of my fellow students. However, I had a lot of company in my mid-20s because former service men, with the GI Bill paying our way, swelled the student body.

I enrolled in the UA Business School, picking up on my studies at Virginia and anticipating a career in sales or marketing.

Before leaving Virginia for the Army I soon would have progressed to a full golf scholarship. When I was at Alabama there were no golf scholarships. I re-established ties with SAE fraternity, soon felt at home on the campus and was only 60 miles or so from Birmingham.

The Athletic Department had made known it would sponsor a golf team and invited prospects to step forward. Through golf in Birmingham and Tuscaloosa, I had already met golfers Buddy Walker and Gene Williams, so I had an early foot in the door. Malcolm Laney, former Woodlawn High School coach, was assigned to be the Athletic Department's representative (not coach) for golf. I established ties with Laney and soon became the golf team's unofficial liaison with him.

In addition to Walker, Williams and me, on the 1946 golf squad were Billy O'Connor, Read Northen, Harry Brock and Jim Head. Team members were chosen on the basis of scorecards in several competitive rounds.

Thanks to support from Harry Pritchett, a pre-war UA golfer and one of this state's best in later years, we had playing privileges at Tuscaloosa Country Club and unofficial coaching help from Pritchett. Each team member worked to improve his game with suggestions from the other players.

OUR TEAM'S WIN-LOSS RECORD probably was around .500. We were not world-beaters, but we had good individual performances in 1946 and '47. We participated in the Southern Intercollegiate Golf Tournament held in those years at Athens, Ga. I made the first flight one year, losing 2 and 1 to a Florida player.

In a UA match with Ole Miss in 1946, my opponent was a promising collegian named Cary Middlecoff of Memphis. For the life of me, I couldn't recall how that head-to-head meeting with Middlecoff came out, so I telephoned him to check on the outcome. Cary said he couldn't remember either but suggested that we settle it on a tie. That suited me. If it isn't recorded elsewhere, here it is: I tied Middlecoff! (Now, if some eager-beaver doesn't check up and find out differently).

One memory of that Ole Miss match that remains clear: The golf course was right next to the track and field facility; occasionally as one of us would start to hit or putt, a starter's gun would go off nearby and interrupt the stroke.

Cary turned pro a few weeks before the 1947 Masters in Augusta and tied for the halfway lead. He fell back after that, but what a debut! He went on to become a Masters and U.S. Open champion (1949). For the Open he won $2,000; today a caddy at the Open probably would earn that much.

When the UA team made ready for one of its infrequent road trips, I would go to Coach Laney (the title was from football, not golf) to get expense money. Because golf wasn't high on the Athletic Department priority list, we would get a few dollars each, plus golf balls and gloves that manufacturers had donated.

Gasoline and food costs were supplemented, not paid for, out of the advances from Laney. Harry Brock's dad was a gasoline distributor, so he had an ID we could use to get gas, and in those lean years, that was a welcome plus. For the record, Brock became a good golfer.

Once after a match in Dothan, we went to the hotel desk next morning to check out and found that we couldn't pay the bill. The manager asked us to leave our equipment as hock, but by calling Laney we convinced the manager that the University would stand good for us.

Before a trip, team members would give me a list of classes they would miss and I would get excuses from the Athletic Department for our instructors. We took textbooks on trips but I doubt they were used much.

IN FEBRUARY 1946 I met pro golfer and former major league baseball player Sam Dewey Byrd, and from that meeting on, my golf career took a decided turn for the better.

Born in Bremen, Ga., Byrd had moved to Birmingham and spent what time he could here. His wife was Rachel "Rae" Smith, a former Miss Birmingham.

Byrd had played eight major league seasons as an outfielder with the New York Yankees and the Cincinnati Reds. He got into pro golf even before he left baseball and finished in the top five in the 1941 and '42 Masters. He won the 1944 Philadelphia Open, the wartime equivalent of the U.S. Open, and earned Byron Nelson's salute as perhaps the greatest-ever long-iron player.

Byrd became pro at Detroit's Plum Hollow Club, played the winter pro circuit in Florida and usually stopped over in hometown Birmingham en route back to Detroit. He and Rae would visit relatives in East Lake.

Industrialist William "Bill" McWane, a golf fan and strong supporter of my efforts, called and asked me if I would like to meet and play a round with Byrd at Birmingham Country Club. Would I ever! Just being on the course with this star athlete was thrill enough, but Byrd provided icing by critiquing my game after our round.

Bill McWane won the Alabama Lefthanded Golf Championship in the 1950s. Even though he was somewhat older than I was, we became close friends. When he was president of the Southern Golf Association, I served as secretary-treasurer, and I learned a lot about administration from him.

Byrd told me he saw potential in my play, but that if I wanted to progress,

I had to make changes in my swing. He was candid about my weaknesses, but he sensed my desire to be a good golfer. He promised to help me, as time permitted, but told me not to play any more competitive matches except those I was already committed to play at Alabama. I readily agreed.

Byrd told me I was "too flippy" with my hands, that I used excessive hand motion. He emphasized also that I had a mechanical problem in not using a larger portion of my body; I did not have a big enough shoulder turn, he said.

A golf swing begins in the feet, Byrd preached; if my feet were not braced, I wouldn't put my body to full use in the turn of my swing.

On the other side, Byrd emphasized that I had to create a swing with its component parts, allowing me to be consistent. One component: Make sure the club face is square when it returns to the ball. He wanted me to have a swing that, even if I didn't hit the ball properly, I would still be in the fairway. Today people still tell me that I missed my last fairway "about 1929."

Byrd didn't develop me into a long ball hitter; he taught me how to be a very straight hitter, as he was.

Over the years ahead I developed a knack of getting out of tight spots because Byrd taught me how to come out. Sometimes he would drop balls in the woods, perhaps behind a tree, then discuss the options of getting out. If I had to clear an overhanging limb, for example, he would have me close the face of the club to reduce the loft of the ball.

ON THE 1947 ALABAMA TEAM with me, after tryout rounds, were Gene Williams, Buddy Walker, Read Northen, Bill O'Connor, Harry Brock, Billy Jamison, Jim Head, Jr., and Arthur Gamble.

In that still-postwar era, our team arranged some of our matches with other college teams in what might be described as a flukey arrangement; outright subterfuge, to be candid. We would arrange to play as individual competitors, but also as a team by matching opposing collegians by scorecards, precisely as if we were on a college course. As I said, flukey, but it benefitted both the college teams and the host clubs.

Along with attending summer school in 1947, I landed a job as golf bag salesman for Burton Manufacturing of Jasper. I made a grand total of $160 in commissions — and got into trouble.

I received a letter from the United States Golf Association asking if I had

1947 Alabama Golf Team (left to right): Read Northen, Harry Brock, Billy Jamison, Elbert Jemison, Gene Williams and Arthur Gamble. Not shown are Buddy Walker, Billy O'Connor and Jim Head, Jr. (University of Alabama photo.)

been selling golf bags and if so, did I get the sales job based on my golfing skill or reputation. I responded, yes, to which the USGA answered that I was in technical violation of the amateur status rule. Agreeing not to do it again, I was excused without penalty.

Years later, as chairman of the USGA Executive Committee's Amateur Status Committee, I saw in USGA files the report of my "violation." I showed it to my amused USGA colleagues.

OF THE MANY POSITIVE THINGS that happened to me at the University, the best was meeting Jess Ann Yarbrough of Huntsville, a pretty member of Delta Delta Delta Sorority. We soon grew fond of each other and the relationship led to marriage in November 1949 (wedding details later in this account).

The possibility that I might resume a military career or turn pro golfer dimmed because Jess Ann frowned on both. But the ideas still gnawed at me.

I went to summer school in 1947, coming home on weekends to play golf at Highland and Roebuck, then returned to regular classes in the fall. My only golf activity at the Capstone that fall was playing friendly matches with '47 team members Billy O'Connor, Buddy Walker and Gene Williams.

By then the money I had saved during the war was exhausted. I had been on my own five years and I didn't want to ask for help from my family again. The GI Bill wasn't sufficient to tide me over. Also, I wanted to test myself as an amateur golfer by competing in open tournaments.

MY TWO YEARS AT THE UNIVERSITY had been most rewarding and a half century later I still treasure my time there. I had made countless friends, especially in golf circles, and later I renewed and enhanced many of those friendships. In the years after UA I couldn't go 30 miles without running into someone I had met at college.

In those post-UA years an amateur could enter almost any open by writing ahead to tournament officials, showing up and paying a modest qualifying fee, as low as $5.

I played tournaments in places like Anniston, Selma and Montgomery and concluded that I was not yet skilled enough to win tournaments. I was only a reasonably good college golfer at that time.

In the late 1940s I went down to try qualifying for the New Orleans Open. If you weren't a bona fide tour player, you could play a round hoping to qualify for the last 10 places in the tournament.

Fifty or 60 of us competed for those 10 places and by the time I teed off late in the day I realized that darkness might catch me on the course. Sure enough it did and I asked Clayton Heafner, the pro with whom I was paired in that round, what I should or could do. Exempt as a tour regular, Heafner didn't have to finish that round, but he helped me finish and qualify in a somewhat unusual manner.

"I can't see down the fairway," I said.

"Don't worry," Heafner reassured me. "Even if you bogey these last two holes, you'll probably qualify. I'm going out a couple hundred yards on the fairway and strike a match. You just hit toward the match."

I saw the light — literally. I bogeyed that hole and with Heafner's next match, along with help from the clubhouse lights, bogeyed the long par-4 18th and qualified!

Robert Ripley's "Believe It or Not" could have used that feat; playing golf by matchlight.

8
Decisions, Decisions

The money I had saved in Europe was now exhausted. The college GI Bill didn't pay for my golf balls and gasoline. Now at age 26 after I had been self-sustaining for the previous five years, I wasn't about to ask my family for financial help.

Thus, I left the University short of my degree. I vowed I would complete it one day, but I simply haven't yet found the time to do so.

I was poised, confident and adequately prepared, I told myself, to compete in the marketplace and on the fairways.

I thought I had resolved, before leaving the University, that turning professional was not the route for me. But I was still nagged by the thought that I should at least give the pro tour a try.

Nevertheless, the question of where I would work had first priority. Jemison Realty Co., where Uncle Bob and Dad would have welcomed me, just didn't seem the right choice, not with my itch to make it on my own without family help. Where then?

Several businesses contacted me with job feelers. Among executives who wanted to talk with me were President John Coleman of Birmingham Trust National Bank (now SouthTrust), President John Persons of First National Bank (now AmSouth) and President Jimmy Lee of Buffalo Rock-Pepsi

Bottling Co. Coca-Cola officials in Huntsville, who knew of my relationship with Jess Ann Yarbrough of Huntsville, also indicated they wanted to talk to me.

Because of my contact with Coca-Cola people in Huntsville, I had become interested in the marketing of Coke. Moreover, the Jemisons and Crawford Johnsons, who owned the Birmingham franchise, were longtime friends and Dad owned a little Coca-Cola stock. So, had I been approached by the Johnsons, I would have interviewed there. But the call never came and the possible relationship never developed.

I deeply appreciated the interest of all who contacted me, but I had two reservations about their feelers: (1) I believed they would involve me largely in public relations because of my participation in golf and (2) I wanted to pursue a possible career in insurance.

Why insurance? Because in that field my earnings would depend almost entirely on me, on my confidence and ability. So I began to look around

ONE DAY AFTER TALKING possible employment with my good friend Arthur Crowder of the Prudential Insurance company in the old Comer Building, I was on the down elevator with three former Auburn football players, Clarence Grimmett, Gus Pearson and Bo Russell. I knew them all and knew that they were with MassMutual, one of the nation's leading life insurance companies.

"What are you doing?" Grimmett asked me in obvious reference to employment.

"Nothing yet."

"Then how about going back up with us to see our general agent, Frank Drake?"

I agreed, so when we reached the lobby, we rode back up to the MassMutual offices.

Frank Drake, who knew my family and my golf background, wasn't a great student of insurance, but he had a winning personality and was a dynamic leader, a man's man.

We went straight to the points we wanted to make. When I asked him what he would pay me, he replied, "Whatever you're worth. A lot if you're worth a damn." Capsuled, his pitch to me was, "This is a great company and a great opportunity for you. Take it or leave it."

A blunt approach like that might have turned off some people, but it had the opposite effect on me; it turned me on. And very soon I went to work for MassMutual. I wanted to make it or fall on my own. To me, that wasn't being cocky. It was self-confidence.

Sam Byrd's tutoring continued to result in gradual improvement of my golf.

I would get with Byrd any time it was convenient for him. The convenience was comprised largely of his stopovers in Birmingham when he was Florida-bound for winter pro tournaments and on the return trip to his club pro position at Detroit's Plum Hollow Country Club.

Sam would phone or write, saying when he would be in Birmingham to visit his family in East Lake, usually for two or three days, and I would arrange to meet him.

He never charged me a penny for his tutoring. I think he had decided I had the potential to become a good golfer and he seemed to get pleasure watching my improvement.

His lessons included homework to be done until his next visit. For example, to help me stop being "flippy" with my hands, he had me do a particular drill over and over. When I hit with a 7-iron, he had me choke down the club a little; that way, he said, it was easier for me to keep my hands out of my swing. To achieve better balance, he had me use my feet and legs more.

Byrd taught me that when I got into tense circumstances in which I had to play well I had to rely on my swing and not try anything new or tricky. So I envisioned the Byrd swing and that helped me make successful shots. Slowly but surely my game was improving and my confidence growing, thanks in large measure to Byrd.

Not everyone agreed with Byrd's teaching. Years later, after I had won my first state championship, a golfer friend remarked, "You were a better golfer before Byrd got hold of you." I disagreed heartily. "The truth is," I replied, "I never was able to win a state championship before Byrd taught me."

THIS POINT NEEDS STRESSING: It was not my aim to produce insurance sales for MassMutual by playing golf. I was in insurance, I played golf, the business happened. In any sales field, the more people you meet the more likely you are to be productive. I was fortunate through golf to meet many people who were good enough to do business with me.

It's true that most people who have the money to play golf usually have the wherewithal to buy insurance. It's also true that some people play too much golf and don't have money for anything else.

As I indicated earlier, my boss, Frank Drake, wasn't a great student of insurance, but he was a dynamic and resourceful leader. He knew about my promoting golf at the University of Virginia, in the Army and at the University of Alabama. He knew that I had helped organize golf teams and had been an unofficial coach.

So Drake decided to involve me in organizing and promoting exhibitions, especially events that would help raise money for charities. He knew that MassMutual would benefit, at least peripherally. If news media did not mention the company name, a simple statement such as "Jemison is a sales executive for an insurance company" would be a plus for MassMutual.

Starting as a sales agent, I had moved up to agency supervisor. That meant I was active in two areas: management and sales production. I had representatives under my supervision in towns like Selma and Cullman. I was still writing business, but after a while I realized that my management position curtailed my personal production time and cramped my golf. I could make reasonably good money in sales and still play golf. For a time I could deduct golf expenses for tax purposes, then the IRS put an end to that.

GOLF EXHIBITIONS, usually pitting a big-name pro and talented amateur against another pro-amateur team, were big drawing cards in the late 1940s. Looking back, it's easy to see why.

Pro golf tournaments were getting excellent play on newspaper sports pages, but television exposure was still a few years ahead. The pro tournament schedule favored large cities with their big-crowd potential, so mid-size cities like Birmingham welcomed an opportunity to see pro stars, if only one or two at a time. Organizations such as the American Cancer Society were well rewarded when they arranged a pro-amateur exhibition.

Naturally the local amateurs who teamed with pro stars also benefitted, playing before large turnouts and picking up pointers from the pros. My greatest benefit from playing in pro-amateur exhibitions was learning to withstand the limelight and play with confidence before large galleries.

Golf was moving into a growth era, even before the arrival of Arnold Palmer and Jack Nicklaus. Pro headliners were people like Byron Nelson, Ben Hogan, Sam Snead, Sam Byrd, Harold "Jug" McSpaden, Ed "Porky" Oliver and Clayton Heafner.

Bill Campbell, later president of the United States Golf Association, was a top amateur. In the South were Arnold Blum of Macon, Ga.; Billy Joe Patton of North Carolina, who almost won the Masters in 1954; Dale Morey of North Carolina and LSU, and Sonny Ellis of Columbus, Ga.

Somewhere back in the pack but beginning to make a move was Elbert S. Jemison, Jr.

Even after working in the insurance business several months I still had not totally dismissed the possibility of trying to play on the pro golf tour. Participating in exhibitions with pros, entering invitational tournaments and local and sectional amateur tournaments would help resolve the lingering question.

In 1947 I played an exhibition in Huntsville with Herschel Spears, talented assistant pro to Charley Hall at Birmingham Country Club, as my partner. Our opponents were Bob Lowry, Sr. and Jr., whom I had gotten to know on my trips to Huntsville to see Jess Ann.

Spears shot a sizzling 63, which helped us win with ease. He once hit more greens in a Masters Tournament than did the eventual Masters winner. But he was a terrible putter.

Herschel and I were good friends and I used him as a trainer or sparring partner, to borrow from boxing. We often played nine holes late in the day with Herschel, a better golfer, giving me 1-1/2 holes up. With that advantage I was able to swap out winning the nine-hole matches.

But when Spears was on, he was unbeatable. Once at Birmingham Country Club, he birdied the fourth hole, looked at me and said, "Now I'll give you five more (birdies) just like that." And darned if he didn't. He birdied 5, 6, 7, 8 and 9 and wiped me out that day!

In 1948 I managed my first major golf exhibition. Played at Birmingham Country Club for benefit of the Jefferson County Chapter of the American Cancer Society, the event featured Lloyd Mangrum, former U.S. Open champion. Sam Byrd, who knew Mangrum on the pro tour, helped me line him up for the exhibition.

Mangrum didn't disappoint, shooting 68. Herschel Spears had 71; Scudday Horner of Montgomery and Byrd both shot 73. That exhibition proved to be a launching pad for many such events I would manage in the years ahead.

Among the tournaments I played in back then were the Southern Amateur in Louisville, the St. Petersburg Open (where "Porky" Oliver and other name pros competed), the New Orleans and Atlanta Opens and the Gulf Coast Open in 1948, where I was low amateur and, as I recall, fifth lowest including the pros.

Had I been a pro in the Gulf Coast event, I think my fifth-place finish would have netted me about $450, an amount not to be scoffed at in those years, but then again not a purse that would have done much for my bank account after expenses were deducted.

AS MENTIONED, I CONTINUED improving under Sam Byrd's direction, but he was forever looking for other ways to polish my game. Johnny Revolta, generally considered golf's best short-game player in those years, was pro at the Gulf Hills Dude Ranch in Ocean Springs, Miss., and a close friend of Byrd. So Sam seized the opportunity to have me come under Revolta's tutelage.

Byrd and Revolta arranged for a Sunday exhibition at Gulf Hills, prior to which Revolta would check out my short game. Sam and I arrived in Ocean Springs on a Friday and I went to the practice tee. Revolta taught me points about golf that I'd never encountered.

For example: How to loft a ball higher and still come down softer. Also, when to close the face of a pitching wedge to create a lower trajectory (called "quail high") and still have a spin to stop the ball. That's a handy auxiliary shot when hitting under limbs or over a sand bunker. I wish I could still execute such shots.

Speaking of sand, Byron Nelson once told me that hitting a sand shot was the only time you should keep weight on the right foot as you hit through the ball.

Sam and I played a practice round with Revolta on Saturday, then in a payback for Revolta's tutoring, we played the exhibition Sunday.

Obviously the participants were pleased after a 1950s exhibition at Ocean Springs, Miss. Left to right:
Mickey Bellande, Jemison, my tutor Sam Byrd and Sam's good friend Johnny Revolta.

Thus I was benefitting from tutoring by two of golf's leading pros, Byrd and Revolta. Not many aspiring young amateurs like me could enjoy that level of assistance.

In 1949 I made one of my best showings to date playing in the Birmingham Invitational Tournament, probably second only to the state ama- teur tournament as toughest to win. I lost in the championship match 1-up to Nelson "Buddy" DeBardeleben. *Birmingham Age-Herald* sports editor Bob Phillips wrote that our match produced some of the finest golf the Birmingham Invitational had seen in years. I confess that after that perfor- mance I had visions of one day winning the state amateur championship.

Cary Middlecoff, who only three years before had been on the Ole Miss team that our Alabama team played, came to Birmingham's Roebuck Club in the spring of 1949 to play an exhibition for the Jefferson County Chapter of the American Cancer Society. Almost overnight Cary had become a big name on the pro tour and we were fortunate to have him in Birmingham.

Leading citizens supported the charity event by paying big money for tickets, among them industrialist/philanthropist Erskine Ramsay. Already having bought a ticket for $500, Mr. Ramsay agreed to pay $1,000 for a second ticket — if he could get a kiss from each of several pretty girls helping us. They kissed. He paid.

We deferred to the grand old man in another way: For some reason he liked "round corners" on printed matter, so we had our tickets rounded off. Mallie Moughon, daughter of Bill Moughon and wife of Glenn Ireland, was ticket chairman. By the way, Moughon was one of Alabama's finest-ever putters.

Herschel Spears and I were paired against Middlecoff and M.G. Walker.

Cary Middlecoff (far right) was the main attraction for a cancer benefit at Roebuck Golf Club in 1949. Left to right: Herschel Spears, Jemison, Alabama football star Harry Gilmer (exhibition referee), M.G. Walker, and philanthropist Erskine Ramsay.

It was a close match with Middlecoff-Walker coming out on top. Middlecoff shot a 70, Spears 73, Walker 74, Jemison 75.

Handling the Middlecoff exhibition event launched me into serious participation in the "other side" of golf: administration. That topic will be dealt with in detail later in this text.

After the exhibition, Middlecoff and his father, a Memphis dentist who came down for the event, encouraged me to join the pro tour. Such encouragement rekindled my interest, but only temporarily.

PERHAPS THE MOST MEMORABLE exhibition I played in involved the great Ben Hogan. Not only was I given responsibility for arranging the exhibition, but also I had the pleasure of being paired with Hogan.

Frank Drake, my boss at MassMutual, again assisted the Jefferson County Chapter of the American Cancer Society in 1951. Aware of Hogan's success on the pro tour and of his crowd-drawing power, Drake asked me to try lining him up for a Birmingham exhibition to benefit the Cancer Society. He had recovered from a traffic collision that almost killed him.

I learned that Hogan was to be guest on a Bob Crosby television show in New York the week I would be en route to an insurance school in Springfield, Mass. We decided I should try to see Hogan at the show and talk about a Birmingham charity exhibition.

Confirming where the Crosby show would be, I went to the alley near the theater stage door. Without a ticket, I had to watch for an opportunity to enter through that door — and made it. Once inside, the first person I encountered was Crosby. He was the warm, easy-to-meet person TV audiences knew. I told him about meeting his brother Bing in Europe during World War II; I'm sure that didn't hurt my mission.

I told Bob why I was there, he introduced me to Hogan's wife, Valerie, and told me to go backstage with her after the show.

Everything worked like a charm. Introduced to Hogan, I told him what I was there for, and he agreed to play the charity exhibition in Birmingham. We exchanged phone numbers so we could iron out details.

The match was played July 7 at Roebuck, green with belatedly planted ryegrass that looked decorative, I suppose, but got a chuckle from Bantam Ben because ryegrass is not normally grown in July.

Before teeing off at Roebuck in 1951. Left to right: Herschel Spears, Elbert Jemison, Paul Stapp and Ben Hogan.

Hogan and I were matched against Herschel Spears and Paul Stapp, my amateur counterpart. Was I awed to be teamed with one of golf's alltime greats? Absolutely. But I was confident, too, eager to play well before a home crowd.

My confidence was sorely tested on the first hole — not by the way I played, but by a Hogan question. As Ben walked up to hit his second shot, he asked me what club he should use. Was he in earnest or just being nice to his amateur partner? I had never seen him play and that led to a bad guess. I suggested his 6-iron; he used it and hit well over the green. The great man didn't ask my advice again.

Despite the ryegrass, which made putting a challenge, Hogan shot 68, Spears 72, Stapp and I 74s. Alf Van Hoose of *The Birmingham News* wrote that I "hit as many spectacular shots as Hogan did but couldn't tap the ball home with the same authority as his partner."

All told, the exhibition was a success, attracting about 3,000 spectators and netting a tidy sum for the Jefferson County cancer chapter. Van Hoose later said he believed the exhibition gallery was the largest ever in Alabama up to that time.

Hogan was staying at the Tutwiler Hotel, then at Fifth and 20th, and we had dinner there that night.

Hogan sometimes has been described as cold and hard to know. I was with him on several occasions after the exhibition, and I can vouch that once he sized up a person, he became warm and friendly.

In a recent year I boarded a plane on which Hogan was a passenger headed for the Masters in Augusta. He invited me to sit by him and we reminisced about the exhibition. He told me he didn't anticipate playing much longer (he didn't), but people still flocked to see him everywhere he went. Some regard him as golf's greatest-ever. I see him as one of the greatest.

Whether he was playing or practicing, Hogan always sought perfection. He was like a skilled surgeon at work, focused on what he was doing and not interested in conversation. Off the golf course and one on one, he was a pleasure to be with. I consider myself fortunate to have played golf with Hogan. He died in 1997.

IN THE YEARS SINCE leaving the University of Alabama and working in insurance, I had tested the waters in golf, trying to decide once and for all whether I should try the pro tour.

The advantages of touring were obvious: (1) traveling the United States and perhaps beyond; (2) relishing the challenge of top competitors; (3) taking a shot at high-income opportunities; (4) establishing lasting relationships with fellow professionals.

The disadvantages, too, were obvious: (1) traveling without letup; (2) living in motel rooms; (3) wild-card and mostly unbalanced meals; (4) living away from home and family; (5) facing uncertain income and constant pressure to win.

For me, the liabilities outweighed the benefits. Having tested the waters, I was breaking clean: No pro tour for me. I would content myself with playing in local, state and regional tournaments; I would enter qualifying for the National Amateur; I would play exhibitions when invited. And always there would be the fun of local club tournaments.

I was well into a rewarding business career that afforded opportunity to meet touring pros and top amateurs.

A factor that influenced me was my increasing participation in golf administration. I had dabbled in it in college at Virginia and Alabama. But I had no inkling that one day I would be asked to serve at the highest level, in this country and abroad. Being an administrator had its own rewards.

9
Meet the Family

To rehash a line from the Good Book: Golf giveth and golf taketh away. Especially in regard to the family. The game has rewarded me handsomely in a variety of ways. And I have shared the rewards — the championships, the fun trips, the people I've met — with my family.

My participation as both competitor and administrator has often cost me valuable time with my wife and children. This account would not be accurate without that acknowledgement.

My years of playing golf, along with participating in administration, in the long run consumed more time than I was aware of then. But once on the USGA Executive Committee and on the state and Southern boards (more than three decades), I earnestly felt I was making an important contribution. And I enjoyed it. But in retrospect, I was away from home too much.

There was an upside. My lifestyle resulted in interesting experiences and enjoyment for family members. They met people and went many places because of my involvement in golf.

Do I seek now to explain it all away? No. Only to acknowledge the lost time and to hope that I have made at least partial amends by sharing the rewards.

I FIRST SAW Jess Ann Yarbrough across a crowded room at a University of Alabama fraternity-sorority gathering. It wasn't the proverbial love at first sight, but it definitely was interest at first sight. Sufficient interest to ask a bystander who she was, and later in a library, remembering she was from Huntsville, to scribble "47-tag?" on paper and hold it for her to see. I hoped the reference to a Madison County auto license would lead to a full introduction. Luckily it did.

Jess Ann struck me as an All-America type. She had been a cheerleader at Huntsville High School, was popular among sorority sisters and, as I quickly learned, was poised and intelligent.

She knew little about golf, but I worked to change that. I invited her out to watch our University golf team practice.

Before long Jess Ann took me to Huntsville to meet her family. They were a close family, living in a comfortable large brick, English-style home and I noted from the outset that her parents were warm and gracious.

Following tradition back then, I decided to ask Mr. John B. Yarbrough for permission to marry his daughter. He was a fun guy affectionately called "Major Hoople." He loved to fish but didn't play golf. He attended Kiwanis Club meetings and played poker one night a week with close friends.

I had gone to the Yarbrough home for Sunday dinner and soon after I made my pitch. "Mr. Jack, I need to talk to you."

"Well, hurry up," he said. "I'm going fishing."

So I hurried up and told him Jess Ann and I wanted to get married. He said we had his blessing and hurried away to meet his fishing partner.

FORTUNATELY, THE YARBROUGHS took a liking to me from my first visit. Jess Ann's brother, John, was a military type like me, only he was in the Regular Army. Born in 1924, he had been graduated from the Gulf Coast Military Academy and attended Auburn. He had served in the war in Europe with the 26th Infantry Division as an officer in the Corps of Engineers. He remained in the service as Regular Army. He is retired and lives in Hampton, Va., with his wife, Belle, and a large number of family members in the area. He is a wonderful brother-in-law.

Jess Ann's older sister, Helen, was married to Nathan Porter, who had just gotten out of the Navy. She died a few years ago.

A younger sister, Minnie Lois, is married to George Neal. They live in Huntsville, which enables us to see them often.

The Yarbroughs had a large ante-bellum home on nearby Monte Santo Mountain that they occupied every summer. It was a fun place to visit and the site of many family fun gatherings.

Back then, before the space people moved in, Huntsville had about 20,000 citizens. It's hard to believe now, but the town had only a nine-hole golf course. I suppose that was indicative of what the citizenry thought of golf: apparently only a few people played.

Jess Ann soon got a taste of what golf on the road was like when in 1948 she, her mother and an aunt accompanied me when I competed in the Gulf Coast Open in Gulfport, Miss. Jess Ann had to hide her dog, Mister, in the cottage closet because the place didn't allow pets.

WE WERE MARRIED on Nov. 5, 1949, at the beautiful old First Presbyterian Church, Huntsville, with a reception at the Yarbrough home.

Jess Ann's attendants were her sister Helen Yarbrough Porter, matron of honor; sister Minnie Lois Yarbrough, maid of honor; my sister Jeanie Jemison; sister-in-law Belle Yarbrough, Margaret Burton, Sara Thiemonge, Jane Lehman and Jane Grote.

My father was best man. Groomsmen were Henry G. "Buzz" Seibels, Jr. of Birmingham; Pres Bradford, a friend from University of Virginia years; Bob Ramsay of Birmingham; John Yarbrough, Jess Ann's brother; Alex Hunter, fellow insurance man, and Charlie Nice, a future Birmingham judge.

We hid our getaway car at a plantation home about 10 miles out of town. We spent our first night in Chattanooga, then drove next day to the Sedgefield Inn near Greensboro, N.C.

If Jess Ann had had doubts about marrying a golfer, she had reinforced doubt the next morning. When she woke, she walked to a window and saw a golf green; she walked to an opposite window and saw another green. She had spent her second night as Mrs. Jemison on a golf course!

From Greensboro we caught a plane for New York, saw the sights and danced to the music of Vaughan Monroe's orchestra.

OUR FIRST HOME was an $11,000 bungalow on Euclid Avenue; the

Our wedding . . . a joyous occasion.

down payment was $2,000 and monthly payment $61. If my memory isn't faulty, golf balls at the time were about 40 cents and Cokes still a nickel.

Jess Ann settled right in to meal planning by cooking steaks every night. She soon made adjustments and the menu expanded.

Our new lifestyle didn't last. The Korean War began in June 1950 and as a National Guard officer with the 31st Dixie Division, I was called to duty.

I had injured my ankle during service in World War II and X-rays showed a calcium deposit still in the ankle. The Army insisted that I sign a waiver concerning my ankle, I refused to do so, and we were soon back home.

THE DECADE THAT HAD just begun would be referred to as the Fabulous Fifties, and the Jemisons could identify, in a sense, with that description.

My production at MassMutual was steadily improving as was my golf. If there has been a "most successful" competitive era for me, surely it was the 1950s; that decade will be dealt with in an ensuing chapter. But more rewarding than golf or business, we welcomed a daughter into our family in the '50s and two sons in the 1960s. As all proud parents know, it's a new and far more meaningful life when children join the scene.

The arrival of Anne Sevier Jemison in 1957 was an exciting and joyous occasion in our home. A bright, perky child, Anne would grow up to be an excellent student who loved the outdoors, especially riding horses.

Exempt from final exams as a Mountain Brook High School senior, for a year she attended Mount Vernon College in Washington, D.C., transferred to Auburn as a sophomore, then got political fever and returned to Mount Vernon to major in political science her third and fourth college years.

After graduation, Anne worked for the Federal Election Commission for almost a year, then joined Alabama Sen. Jeremiah Denton's staff, writing speeches and doing public relations work. Denton said she was his best staffer "because she would tell me when I was wrong."

After George Bush became vice president, he called Denton's office asking for Anne. "She's in a meeting," a staffer answered. "May I tell her who is calling?"

"This is George Bush."

"Yeah, right, George Bush. Ha-ha."

But it was Bush. The future president explained later that he wanted to

Anne S. Jemison, 1978 Beaux Arts Krewe Queen.

tell Anne that if she left Denton's staff, she would be welcome on the Bush staff.

In 1981 Anne met Rest Heppenstall, member of a prominent Pittsburgh family. They married in 1983. They have two children, Rest Baker Heppenstall, Jr., known as Baker, 12, who plays golf, soccer and baseball, and Jess Anne, 9, who plays soccer, loves horses and competes in local shows.

Rest is a fine golfer who came from a golfing family. His father was seven times club champion of Fox Chapel Golf Club in Pittsburgh and prominent in Pennsylvania golf affairs. His mother also was an ardent golfer. He has a brother, Bob, Jr., a golf enthusiast who is a Presbyterian minister. He and his wife, Pattie, and their four children live in the Fox Chapel area of Pittsburgh.

Rest is a wonderful husband, dedicated father, and fun golf partner — what more could a father-in-law want? Jess Ann and I are pleased that Anne, Rest, Baker and Jess live near us.

ELBERT S. JEMISON, III, known familiarly as Bo, was born in 1962. His interest in sports and recreation surfaced in elementary school, where he played softball and flag football, then in camping and fishing.

Bo showed an early interest in golf, joining me on the course, then for a couple of years in the Southeastern Father-Son Championship event at the Anniston Country Club. A memorable occasion was the year we made our way to the championship round, where we played the Cantrells of Gadsden.

What a match! We were even after the regulation 18 holes and began a sudden-death playoff — "sudden" is the key word in such a playoff because usually only a hole or two is required. With a 2-stroke-per-hole handicap, Bo once got down in 2, thus scoring a rare 0 (a hole-in-none!). We went eight

*ubilant over a hole-in-none! My partner, Bo, in a Southeastern Father-Son Tournament at Anniston, celebrates
after scoring a gross 2 on a par-3 hole. With a 2-stroke handicap, that comes out a net 0.*

Anniston Star *photo*

Family gathering in our backyard. Back: Jess Ann, Anne, Elbert. Front: Richard (left) and Bo.

Anne and Rest at the beach with Jess and Baker.

extra holes before the Cantrells won.

Bo was active in youth work at the Episcopal Church of the Advent and participated in rafting trips in Tennessee. He earned a degree in criminal justice at UAB.

Richard Rand Jemison was born in 1965. Like Bo, he developed an early fondness for fishing and camping. Although I never tried to push him or Bo into golf, Richard also played some with me, and after Bo reached maximum age in the Father-Son Championship, Richard took his turn in that event.

Richard attended Berry Academy, a branch of Berry College in Rome, Ga. He did well there, went to Auburn a year, then transferred to UAB.

MY PARENTS and my sister Jeanie were my loyal supporters all the way — through my school years, military career and my golf efforts. Because Jeanie is 15 years younger, I took some ribbing that she looked more like my daughter than my kid sister. No matter; Jeanie was my biggest fan, especially when she was in high school.

Keeping golf in the family, Jeanie married a real golf enthusiast, George W. Matthews, Jr., who followed in his father's footsteps and became a prominent oral surgeon. He and Jeanie have four children, one of whom is my dentist.

A fun, jovial golf partner everyone likes to play with, the "Great One," as he is known, never has won a major golf championship, but that's not because he hasn't aspired to win one. No one could have a finer brother-in-law.

Jess Ann's parents, sisters and brother, the best of in-laws, always were totally supportive. They looked after our

My sister Jeanie with husband Dr. George W. "Buzzy" Matthews, Jr.

At Mentone with my grandchildren, Baker and Jess.

With my boys: Richard, son-in-law Rest Heppenstall, Bo and grandson Baker.

children while Jess Ann and I were on the road, and they were always there for us. I hope I made them aware of my appreciation.

Perhaps my involvement in playing and administering golf did provide opportunity for Jess Ann and our children to meet many fine people and to go to places that otherwise wouldn't have been possible. Only because of golf have we had fun in Scotland with the American Walker Cup team, visited the White House Oval Office and made numerous trips to Vail, Colo., to participate in the Jerry Ford Invitational. Our children and grandchildren shared in much of that fun.

Jess Ann went with me to numerous tournaments, including the Anniston Invitational every spring. We had many friends there, including some she had known at the University, so that was one of our favorite trips. When I com-

Baker and Jess Heppenstall with former President Gerald R. Ford at a Jemison family dinner in Birmingham, 1996.

peted in the 1960 National Amateur, Jess Ann took Anne to stay with the Yarbroughs and we enjoyed seeing her relatives in St. Louis.

We had frequent fun outings with six or eight couples, particularly the Mobile Invitational, during which we made the most of that city's great seafood restaurants.

ONE OF OUR MOST REWARDING family outings was the 1976 U.S. Open in Atlanta, won by Alabama's Jerry Pate. As a member of the USGA Executive Committee, I attended USGA meetings there that week in conducting the U.S. Open and joined the family in a week of fun.

I had known Jerry and his parents since he was a youngster in Anniston, so when he sank the clinching putt on the 18th green, we celebrated with a bearhug all America saw on network TV and in newspapers. I was one of the officials assigned to his round.

Aside from the golf outings, we as a family have had great trips to the beach and to the mountains, and have shared fun at home on such occasions as backyard cookouts. We hope there'll be more down the road.

10
The Fifties: Fairways and Boardrooms

My competitive juices were bubbling that August day in 1949 as I teed up for my first National Amateur. My opponent at Rochester, N.Y.'s Oak Hills East was a talented New York State senior. The day had begun wet and would stay rainy, but that was not a new problem; golfers learn to endure weather. When our match was called on the loudspeaker — "Now on the tee, Elbert S. Jemison, Jr., of Birmingham, Ala., and Arthur F. Lynch of Winged Foot, N.Y.," — I got goose bumps.

If I hadn't practiced it the day before, the first hole might have been intimidating. It was a monster opener according to Ben Hogan: 442 yards, slight dogleg to the left, a creek wandering across our path 320 yards from the tee and three towering oaks just back of the green.

A time to panic? Not if Sam Byrd had taught you how to stay calm under pressure, as he had taught me. This national tournament was what I had pre-pared for, hoped for, dreamed of. I had reached a pinnacle and was rubbing shoulders with talented amateurs from all across America. So, I thought, let's get on with it.

After the tough starter and through the first few holes, I managed to take a modest lead. Then experience began paying off for my opponent. He moved ahead and doggedly stayed there, ultimately closing me out at 3 and 2.

My first effort in national competition thus had fallen short, but even so I felt pride in having reached the National and in playing reasonably well. I was disappointed, of course, but far from discouraged.

I decided to stay around and watch the next rounds. Then I had a phone call from Birmingham. Friend and fellow golfer Jim Grimmer, a World War II pilot still in the Air Force Reserve, was coming up "to get in some flying time" and give me a flying ride home.

We took off for home in his cavernous cargo plane. Nearing Pittsburgh we ran into an electrical storm that knocked out the radio and forced Grimmer to land at Smyrna Air Force Base near Nashville. That wasn't a choice place to land, but people there saw that we were in trouble and a few turned on their Jeep lights to help guide us in. After repairs we flew on home, Grimmer to shopping mall planning, Jemison to resume his insurance sales and more golf.

EVERY ATHLETE HAS his prime time, the years when he performs best. Because my golf career covers two categories, competitive and administrative, my most productive years could not be so readily pinpointed as others. But identifying my top competitive years is easy: the 1950s. I counted that 1949 National Amateur, along with a few other 1949 events, as warmup for the Fifties; that's why they're covered in this chapter.

By the spring and summer of '49 Sam Byrd had me believing I could (note, that's could, not would) win any tournament I entered. The one exception was that National Amateur; finishing first there was asking a little much of myself. My realistic goal was to play well and I met that goal.

Playing in the Gadsden Invitational in June, I reached the final against Dick Cline. We were even after 15 holes. Dick eagled 16 and my birdie there left me 1 down. He kept up the pressure with a birdie on 17 to my par and that gave him the title.

The Birmingham National Invitational at BCC attracted skilled golfers from several states, and I set my sights on winning it. I came close. In the first round I defeated Leroy McDavid 6 and 4; in the second, I shot 1 under par and ousted Charles DeBardeleben 5 and 4; in the third I edged good friend Paul Stapp 2 and 1.

That put me in the final against Nelson "Buddy" DeBardeleben, who had

En route to winning the 1952 Birmingham Invitational.

defeated Bill McWane 2 and 1 in the other semifinal. Buddy and I had an exciting match. He shot 72; I was one stroke and one hole behind at the finish. Alf Van Hoose's story in *The Birmingham News* reported that DeBardeleben won "despite some brilliant iron shots by Jemison."

Now, the fifties by year.

1950

My best effort this year was a runner-up finish in the Alabama Amateur to Jimmy Ryan at Greenville. For reader convenience (and mine), my two state championships and two runner-up finishes are covered in the next chapter.

1951

For quite a while, I entered various Alabama club invitational tournaments every year. Travel time was minimal (only Mobile and Dothan were more than a couple hours away) and I — along with Jess Ann when she could make it — would see and often compete with longtime friends.

In 1951 I entered the Anniston Invitational and won the championship by defeating old friend Bob Lowry, Jr., 2 and 1.

1952

Improving each year, I won the Birmingham National Invitational at

Birmingham Country Club, defeating John Rogers of Woodward Country Club in the final.

Bob Phillips reported in the *Birmingham Post-Herald* that I gained an early lead and held it to win. The match ended before hundreds of tense spectators, Phillips wrote, "when first Jemison, then Rogers three-putted the last hole." Both of us were 4-over for the match but it was tense all the way. I had made the final by defeating Paul Stapp in 19 holes, Gilbert Wesley 1-up and H.C. Duke 4 and 3.

Club championships are prized because you're usually competing with people you know best: those you've played with week in and week out, truly home folks. Sometimes club tournaments are even more hotly contested than the better-known state and regional tournaments.

In 1952 I played a memorable Birmingham Country Club home club match with Jim Head, Jr., for the Harris Cup, named for Dr. Buck Harris, a staunch BCC supporter. Head had been a teammate on the University of Alabama golf team.

Going to the 18th hole I was 1-down. Jim was first on the green and appeared to have the hole and the championship won for I was in a sand bunker. My only hope was to hole out from the bunker and force a playoff. Fat chance, but as old friend Charley Boswell later said about his blindness: "It was not in my nature to give up."

I'm sure the spectators gathered around the 18th felt I was just going through the motions when I asked my caddy to remove the flag. I was about 25 yards from the cup when I made my do-or-die attempt from the trap. My ball landed on the green and rolled right into the cup.

Head still could win with a good putt, but he missed and we headed to the tee for a playoff. When we reached the green all even, I resorted to what is known as Walter Hagen gamesmanship to win the day. Putting first, I took a long back stroke, decelerated (unnoticed, I hoped) coming forward and almost sank the putt. Then I commented, loud enough for Head to hear: "God, this green is slow!"

He took the bait and putted 12 or 15 feet past the cup, realizing too late he had been had. "It's not all that slow!" he grumbled. I won when he three-putted.

In defense of my so-called Hagen gamesmanship, the strategy was not original with me.

That year I also played in the first Vestavia Country Club Invitational. Because the course was new, we had to contend with small rocks here and there. But the playing field was level, as they say; everybody had to contend with the pebbles.

Pres Thornton and I made the final, and I remember running up a white flag of sorts. Pres had me one down on the 17th hole, but he was in a sand bunker. I was away, lying 3 over the green and after my fourth shot I was still in the rocks and roots and away. I told Pres, "Hit the green (from the bunker) and I'll concede." He did and I did.

1953

Winning the Jefferson County tournament at Highland Park (now Boswell) was rewarding, in part because I outshot several talented golfers in the final round.

Another dividend of that triumph was having a role in the first broadcast of an Alabama golf event and very possibly the first such broadcast in the South. I believe I can vouch for the Alabama "first"; for the South, I'm not sure.

Lionel Baxter, whom many people will remember as a WAPI executive, and sportscaster Maury Farrell approached the tournament officials about broadcasting the event live. Naturally they wanted approval of the players; we said we were willing if there was no talk while we were making our shots.

Equipment needs for on-location or remote broadcasts have changed radically, I presume. That day, almost half a century ago, WAPI had arranged for Boy Scouts to move its equipment around in two little red coaster wagons! Remembering Highland's (Boswell's) hilly terrain, I've often wondered if the broadcast could have survived a little red wagon turning over.

Jim Head, Jr., led Saturday's first round with an excellent 67. Burt Woods and John Thames had 69s, John Rogers and John Wood 71s, Walter Wood and five others had 73s. John Campbell, Jr., and I shot 74s, far enough back not to even merit mention in a news account.

After the second round Sunday morning, the field was to be divided into two groups with the low 20 to comprise the championship flight for the third and final round.

Having breakfast with entertainer Fred Waring (left) and Sam Byrd. In addition to his "Pennsylvanians"
group, Waring was involved with golf at Shawnee-on-Delaware.

By the time we broke for lunch, John Rogers had a two-stroke lead over
me. He had tacked on a 71 and I had improved to 70. He maintained the lead
through nine holes of the afternoon round, but after 16 he had slipped into a
tie with me. An early finisher, I was on the board at 214. John double-bogeyed
17 and his par on 18 left me the winner by two strokes.

WHATEVER CELEBRATING I did after winning the county title had
to be short. I was due in Asheville, N.C., at breakfast time next morning for
a MassMutual meeting, followed by a company golf tournament.

MassMutual cohorts Malcolm McDonald and Bill Hart went up with me, but I did all the driving. With a late start and no interstates, that meant no sleep for me that night. We made the breakfast meeting, were well fed and cheered on by MassMutual executives.

Then, still without sleep or much rest, we teed up for golf. I surprised myself and I'm sure everybody else by shooting a gross-score 67. So that wasn't a bad two-day effort.

I QUALIFIED FOR the 1953 National Amateur at Oklahoma City. So did Ken Venturi, Gene Littler and Dale Morey. Despite my rising confidence, I knew I was not likely to win the title. Don Nichols of Shawnee, Kan., gave me a 6 and 4 thrashing.

Before my match with Nichols, I had hit warmup shots that caught the attention of Byron Nelson, one of the winningest pros. Nelson told me my swing was much like that of a fellow pro, Sam Byrd. Pleased, I told him I had been tutored by Byrd.

The conversation with Nelson led to our having breakfast together and the start of a warm friendship, especially in later years when he was a pro tour commentator for ABC and I was serving on the United States Golf Association Executive Committee, which puts on the the U.S. Open.

1954

I qualified again for the National Amateur in Detroit, but business conflicts forced me to withdraw, disappointing as that was. An up-and-coming young golfer from Latrobe, Pa., won the tournament, defeating Robert Sweeney 1-up. The winner, as of course you had guessed, was Arnold Palmer.

1955

As so often was the case, I was matched with a friend in the championship match of the 1955 Woodward Golf Club Invitational.

On that occasion the friendly rival was Tommy Nicol and we played a stirring finish. After 16 holes I had managed to take the lead 1-up. Nicol birdied 17 to pull even and we kept up the pace with matching birdies on 18. Nicol appeared to be in trouble on the first extra hole when he pushed his tee shot in the woods, but he hit a miraculous shot to the green and sank a long putt to win the match.

The Mobile Country Club Invitational was one of my favorite tournaments through the years and in 1955 I made one of my best showings there. For example, on Saturday I won matches against two of Alabama's top golfers, Jackie Cummings in the morning and M.C. Fitts in the afternoon.

In the championship match Sunday, Scotty Frazer outlasted me 2 and 1. On the front nine my driver broke and, rather than interrupt the match by getting a replacement driver, I made do with a 3-wood. I managed very well with the substitute although I doubt if the decision helped my mental approach. In any case, no alibis; it was Frazer's day.

1956

Despite my firm decision years earlier not to turn pro, one of the many rewards of amateur tournaments was the opportunity to meet future pro stars. Cary Middlecoff, who had been a collegiate opponent, had quickly earned his spurs as a pro. I played another golfer on his way up in the 1956 Florence Invitational.

The Florence area was special to me because it was Mother's hometown, hence a place I visited often in my early years. In '56 I made it to the final round at Florence and played Mason Rudolph of Clarksville, Tenn., for the championship. Mason Rudolph is a name golfers of my era will remember well because he made a name for himself on the pro tour.

We finished the championship 18 all even, then Mason won on the first playoff hole. Later I was paired with him at Gulfport in his first tournament as a pro. The total purse there was $5,000; had I turned pro, I would have won $500. Today that's small potatoes, but back then it was well worth taking home.

1957

After winning my first Alabama Amateur title (details, next chapter), I went to Florence to fill an earlier commitment to play again in that invitational. I won the medal, then withdrew, as I had previously advised. I expressed my regrets and drove to Huntsville to join Jess Ann and daughter Anne for a family vacation.

Buddy DeBardeleben and I played a return match of sorts in the '57

Winning the Birmingham Country Club National Invitational. I am watching as Buddy DeBardeleben putts with large gallery on hand.

Birmingham National Invitational championship at BCC. As related, he had won in 1949. On the way to the 1957 final, DeBardeleben had eliminated Walter Wood, Sam Dixon and Leroy McDavid. I had defeated Frost Walker, Gene Moor and Buddy Walker.

A large gallery watched us shoot par on the front nine, then I suppose fatigue got both of us on the back nine as we went 4-over. This was our fifth round in three days. On 18, with a chance to close it out, both of us overshot the green and bogeyed to force extra holes.

We stayed even for two more holes, then on the third extra I needed a one-footer to win. "Knock it in, for God's sake," Buddy said. We were ready for it to end and finally it did.

1958

Because I was 1957 state champion, in 1958 I was invited to play in a brand-new and prestigious event in Johnstown, Pa., the Tournament for Amateur Champions at Sunnehanna Country Club. The club's philosophy was expressed in the following:

"The members of Sunnehanna Country Club trade a weekend of warm hospitality for the privilege of watching the best amateur golfers in the world in 72 holes of stroke play."

There were 60 of us, the 50 state champions, plus 10 others including the Canadian and Mexican champions, Western and Southern champions and six other special invitees.

Was I pleased? You bet I was. Imagine competing with the top amateur golfers in the world!

Each participant was guest of a Johnstown family and that was very special, of course. Then the tournament committee started us off with a stag dinner and men-only show. All that and a great golf tournament to come.

I was in very select company and admittedly feeling my oats, as they say. I would like to report that I outshot that field of champions, but I didn't. I had set as a goal finishing in the middle group and I managed to do better than that, finishing in the top third with a 305.

Bill Hyndman of Huntington Valley, Pa., won the tournament.

DOUBLE DUTY IN GOLF I've done, but triple? I've done that, too, but I don't recommend it if you're trying to win a golf tournament.

In 1958 while I was president of the Southern Golf Association, I also was golf chairman at the Birmingham Country Club, where the 1958 Southern was being played. Along with having to see that things ran smoothly, I competed in that Southern, hoping to add to my growing list of championships.

What that meant was checking in very early to be sure the BCC grounds superintendent was on duty, then checking on several other aspects of tournament arrangements to be certain we were ready for the army of golfers who would soon show up. Then I would check on my own tee time and hope all my responsibilities wouldn't prevent my performing well.

To be candid, I simply ran out of gas. I made it to the Southern semifinals, but lost there to old friend Bob Lowry, Jr. Hugh Royer won the other semifinal over Tommy Nicol and in the final, Royer defeated Lowry.

1959

Having repeated as Alabama champion in 1958, I was invited back to the Tournament of Amateur Champions in 1959. This time I was the guest of the Dick Hartman family and again treated royally.

Jess Ann flew up to join me and I will never forget her arrival at the Johnstown airport. When she and three other passengers stepped off the Allegheny Airlines plane, the stop was so brief the crew never turned off the engines. Man, they were outta there!

As it had the year before, Johnstown made us glad all over that we had won our state championships. Again I set my sights on finishing at least in the middle group, and again I topped my expectations, finishing about 20th with another 305. I was especially pleased that I had not scored out of the 70s during the eight competitive rounds in the two years at Johnstown.

Tommy Aaron of Gainesville, Ga., won the 1959 Johnstown event.

Another reward for having won the Alabama state title was being invited to play in the International Four-Ball Tournament at Hollywood, Fla., with Bob Lowry, Jr., as my partner. Being a finalist in the Southern had gotten Lowry invited. We had a great time and finished high; I don't remember exactly where.

1960

Playing again in the International Four-Ball at Hollywood, Fla., Lowry and I played alongside Jack Nicklaus in one of his last amateur tournaments before he turned professional. Lowry and I were paired just before or just behind Nicklaus and Deane Beman, both onetime National Amateur champions, at the Orange Brook Club.

At breakfast before playing the final round, Lowry and I were tied for the lead with Nicklaus and Beman. Someone at a nearby table asked Nicklaus if he and Beman were worried about Jemison and Lowry.

"No," he replied nonchalantly.

"Why not?"

"We've seen their swings," and now he grinned. He was just being jovial, but he radiated confidence. After a few tee shots, we knew why. Nicklaus was awesome. Beman wasn't long, but his short game and putting were superior. For the record, Lowry-Jemison didn't win.

QUALIFYING FOR THE FOURTH TIME for the National Amateur, to be played at St. Louis, I was determined to make a better showing this time. And I did, making it to the third round before bowing out of that 1960 event.

After drawing a first-round bye, I took on the New York Metropolitan amateur champion, Jim Iverson of Siwanoy, N.Y. He was a delightful person and a formidable opponent. I managed to defeat him 1-up on the 20th hole.

Although I continued to play well, in the third round I lost 3 and 1 to John Garrett of River Oaks, Texas. Years later I learned that John had become a prominent surgeon.

I was headed for age 40 in 1960 and I felt that I had made a fairly good showing in the National. Players who qualify today usually are younger than most who qualified in my prime years. When I competed, many of the best players had gone through World War II before getting seriously into golf. Most of us didn't have the early instruction that's available to young players today. Back then there were many good amateurs in their 30s and 40s. That's not the case today; most talented players turn pro by their early or mid-20s.

As I recall the 1960 National, the second and third holes were both par 3, a bit unusual. I also remember that apple trees along the fairways bore ripe fruit and several of us yielded to the temptation to help ourselves to samples.

Jess Ann had accompanied me to St. Louis and we had pleasant visits there with her first cousin, Milton Rand, his wife, Jane, and other relatives and friends.

All four National Amateurs I played in were rewarding, but the 1960 was special. In addition to the satisfaction of competing at the highest amateur level in the country, I established many wonderful and lasting friendships with people from several states.

BACK ON THE HOME FRONT in Birmingham during the 1950s, among the people who became valued friends included Bill Kessler, my long-time physician until retirement; Jess Miller, a fun golf partner and fellow board member of AAA-Alabama; Frank Boyd, another fun golf partner; Gene Howe, now-retired physician; Jim Greer, whom I have known since University of Alabama days, and many, many others including Ed Thomas, who married one of my favorite cousins, Susan Dillard.

11
Back-To-Back
State Titles

The 1950s were my most productive golf years, a decade in which I won two state championships and came close to winning two others. Those were in addition to my 1950s efforts covered in the previous chapter. Although state titles aren't always the hardest to win, there's something very special about being state champion, the best golfer in Alabama, at least in title.

As golfers know, the club invitationals, such as the Birmingham National, often attract top golfers from as many as 15 or 20 states, hence are more competitive than the Alabama Golf Association tournaments that are limited to state residents. But being state champion has a ring like almost no other.

As early as my junior golf days I dreamed of being the best golfer in Alabama. The obvious way to achieve that, I believed, was to win the state championship.

I had long heard that winning at competitive golf was a young man's game. Having served in the Army almost four years, I had used up what might have been productive golf years; I would turn 30 in October 1950. On the other hand, being tutored by pro Sam Byrd had helped to accelerate my game.

1950

I had made considerable progress in 1949 by being runner-up in the Gadsden and Birmingham Invitationals and by qualifying for my first National Amateur. Another highly significant event for me in 1949 was marrying Jess Ann.

So I looked to 1950 with anticipation. The state amateur tournament, to be played in late July at the Gadsden Country Club, looked like a great opportunity to challenge my peers, and believe me there were a gang of 'em, including Gardner Dickinson, Harry Pritchett, Bob Lowry, Jr., Tommy Nicol and Buddy Walker.

I was still in the Army Guard as an infantry captain, and one week of a two-week summer camp coincided with state tournament week. I would be training at Fort McClellan while the tournament was played a few miles away at Gadsden.

What to do about the that conflict? Well, I had a double stroke of luck. The first stroke: Gen. Walter J. "Crack" Hanna was the National Guard general heading up our division. The second stroke: Gen. Hanna was both golf fan and golfer.

The first week of camp, after Guard training each day I would practice at the McClellan golf course. I was playing well and I allowed myself to think I just might win that state tournament. As things developed, I would come tantalizingly close.

During tournament week I would take my golf clothes to Gadsden and change there. In reporting the tournament, Alf Van Hoose of *The Birmingham News* wrote that I was "on leave," and I guess I was, in a way, thanks to Gen. Hanna.

Had I put store in omens, I might have pulled out before teeing off. When caddies were assigned, I noted that mine was drunk. I dismissed him and was assigned another.

Then there was the weather: rainy at the start and rainy throughout the tournament. In football, it's said that mud is the great equalizer. In golf, the rain falls on all alike, but it can be a distracting element if you let it. I didn't.

IN THE EARLY 1950s, when match play was still used, we would qualify for flights on Thursday, play two matches Friday, the quarter and semifinals Saturday, then the finalists would play 36 holes for the championship Sunday, 18 in the morning, 18 in the afternoon.

When Darwin wrote about "survival of the fittest," the species he was describing could have included tournament golfers!

My first-round opponent was Harry Webb of Huntsville, known as "the Road Man" because he traveled so much for his cotton company. I had met him when I began going to Huntsville to see Jess Ann. Harry was always gracious in including me in his golf games.

I managed a 1-up victory over Webb Friday morning, then eliminated Emmitt Cassidy of Gadsden 3 and 2 in the afternoon.

My row didn't get any easier in the quarterfinals Saturday morning, but I edged Harold Wesley of Greenville 1-up after pulling even on the 15th with a 65-foot putt, according to a news story. I don't remember a green being that wide or deep.

In the match of the tournament to that point, Harry Pritchett of Tuscaloosa had outlasted Dothan's Gardner Dickinson in a 21-hole quarterfinal. In the semis I was matched with Pritchett, a role model of mine from University of Alabama golf years. He was a former state champion, our unofficial coach at the University and a recognized golf leader in Alabama.

My good fortune held. I continued to play well and newspaper stories, researched by Wendell Givens, reported that I edged Harry 2-up, putting me in the championship match with Jimmy Ryan of Greenville.

The Birmingham News account of my match with Harry said I had successive 35-foot putts for birdies. I don't remember the birdies, but I do remember Harry putting on his patented "I don't feel like playing" act at the first tee. He would try to convince his opponents he felt bad by taking an aspirin. He would repeat that he felt too bad to play but "would try." Those who knew Harry well paid no attention to his act!

To get to the final, Ryan, 22-year-old University of Alabama golfer, had eliminated Leonard Leach of Gadsden 5 and 4, Joe Headrick of Gadsden 2-up, Walter Wood of Birmingham 4 and 3, and Gordon Smith, Jr., of Mobile 3 and 2. Those were impressive showings, especially the victories over Wood and Smith. If he continued to play that well, he would be a formidable opponent.

THE FIRST THREE DAYS of the tournament had been played in intermittent rain, and now on championship Sunday, both morning and afternoon rounds began in rain.

Had Las Vegas bookies quoted odds on that tournament, I doubt if either Ryan or Jemison would have been given much chance of playing for the championship. However, I had had a good 1949 and knew that I had an outside chance of taking the trophy home. Ryan certainly had shown promise, but he seldom had ventured far from his Greenville base.

Feeling each other out like boxers, we halved the first five holes, but when we had finished the 18-hole morning round, Ryan was 2-up.

The stubborn rain greeted us for the afternoon round but neither of us seemed to let it hamper our play. Ryan won the 19th hole to go 3-up, I countered by taking the 20th, but he kept the pressure on, winning the 22nd and stretching his lead to 4-up at the 27th and to 5-up on the 28th.

The gallery probably sensed the end, but I've never been one to give up. I took the 29th, but lost the 30th. On the 31st, Van Hoose wrote in *The News*, Jimmy hit a wedge shot within 18 inches of the cup "for a certain 4" and "they shook hands."

Thus, my first serious bid for a state championship had fallen just short. I was disappointed but not dismayed. Jimmy had played better golf that day and was a gracious winner.

1957

EVEN THOUGH 1957 IS four decades ago, good memories remain. Aside from golf, the year started in grand style with the arrival Jan. 16 of our first child, Anne Sevier Jemison. As first-time fathers will agree, those were exciting times.

After winning the Vestavia Country Club and Birmingham Invitationals, I looked ahead to my next major event, the state tournament. Winning the highly competitive invitation tournaments gave me the confidence to believe I could win the state.

Mountain Brook Club, site of the championship, provided several advantages for me. The course does not require extreme length, but it does call for being straight, which was known to be one of my strengths.

In 1957 we played on the smaller original greens built in 1929, designed by the outstanding architect Donald Ross. He had been employed by the club's founding committee of which my Uncle Robert Jemison, Jr., was a prominent member.

With the new daughter, I was fortunate not to have to leave Birmingham. And I knew I was playing well.

I was tournament chairman for that 41st annual event, but I was determined not to let that distract me from playing my best. When one is both competitor and official, he relinquishes his duties as official. Despite the loss in the 1950 championship to Jimmy Ryan at Gadsden and a state tournament drought of sorts for six years, I felt confident I could win.

My first round did little to justify that confidence. The three front-runners — Frost Walker, Jr., Jackie Cummings and Bob Lowry, Jr., — had opened with par 71s. My 76, which tied for 16th, didn't ignite Jemison-championship talk.

With a fine 69 following his first-round 73, Walter Wood moved into the second-round lead at 142. Close up were Lowry at 143, Sonny Holt 144, Cummings 145, Dick Spencer, Jackie Maness, Walker and a fellow named Jemison at 147. I had settled down to a 71 in that second round and, although five strokes back, I knew I was at least in the hunt. Defending champion Buddy DeBardeleben was four more back at 151.

Much like a quarterback who gains confidence after completing a pass or two, I felt my swing ease into a good feel of consistency in the second round. Another 71 on Saturday kept me in striking distance of the championship. But I had lots of company as we headed for the home stretch.

When we teed off Sunday, title contenders included some of Alabama's most talented golfers: Bob Lowry, Jr., of Huntsville, who led after three rounds at 217; Jackie Cummings of Tuscaloosa, who was tied with me for second at 218; Walter Wood a stroke back at 219; John Rogers at 220; Billy O'Connor, Jim Head and Jackie Maness at 221.

Several others, including Sonny Holt, Frost Walker, Jr., and Buddy DeBardeleben were still threats.

Grantland Rice of *The News* described my round this way (I'm capsuling): Jemison overtook Lowry on the first hole, birdied the sixth, fell back even with a bogey on the seventh, then turned two under with an eagle on No. 9.

"That eagle broke the tournament wide open," Rice reported. "Jemison

There goes my final putt for a 69 as I win the 1957 state amateur championship at Mountain Brook Club. My longtime caddy, James Reynolds (holding flag), watches the winning putt.

could almost have kicked it around the back nine and still gotten home the winner."

Perhaps so, but I didn't really know how I stood until the last couple of holes.

My final-round 69 clinched the championship; it included the eagle 3 on the par-5 ninth hole, a birdie, a bogey and 15 pars for a 2-under 69. With that kind of round I felt that I had won the title with good golf rather than winning because of poor golf by the other contenders.

My tournament total was 3 over par. The 69 was one of only three during the tournament; the others belonged to Walter Wood and John Rogers.

Bob Phillips of the *Birmingham Post-Herald* reported I had won "with a superb comeback" from my qualifying and first-round 76, which had left me 16th. It was a big year for me, he wrote, as I already had won two top invitationals at Birmingham and Vestavia country clubs.

Responding to a Phillips question, I replied, "Yes, it was the finest competitive round I've ever played."

And to another question: "I've at least learned to play golf with my head as well as my hands."

PERHAPS BECAUSE IT WAS my first state title, I recall some aspects of the tournament, thanks in part to Phillips, secretary of the Alabama Golf Association. Phillips reminded me later that I had missed only one fairway, the 14th, and that by only two feet and had not had a 3-putt green during the four rounds.

On the last round at the par-5 ninth hole, caddy James Reynolds had insisted I hit a 4-iron second shot instead of a 3-iron. He was right: I hit the green, stopped about 8 feet from the hole, then sank the eagle putt. I was then three shots in the lead.

The 11th hole is a par 5. In those days I could reach it with two good shots. However, before the championship started I had decided not to go for the green as the risk was too great in a stroke-play event. In two of the four rounds I birdied that hole. In the last round several contenders were going for the green and losing ground with bogeys and double bogeys.

On a hole like the 11th, my view is: Get your par and get out of there. It's a small green guarded by Shades Creek in the front. Actually you cross Shades Creek twice. You come to respect holes like that and treat them tenderly. Unfamiliarity can lead to mistakes.

Sam Dixon, son of ex-Gov. Frank Dixon, was a member of the four-man Mountain Brook Club team. With his team leading as he came to the 18th hole, Dixon hit his second shot in the ditch. He could have taken a penalty stroke and two-putted for a six. But Sam was an aggressive, dynamic golfer, and a little heroic in this case. He tried to play his ball, which was partially out of the water, failed to get out and wound up with a fat 9. His teammates were not happy with him as that cost Mountain Brook the team title.

As I headed for the 18th hole on the last round I had a six-shot lead over my closest pursuer, Lowry. This last hole, a par 4, is an almost-90-degree dog-leg at the drive zone with Shades Creek protecting the green. At that time the green was quite small, guarded on each side by deep, dangerous sand bunkers.

I hit my tee shot exactly where I wanted, leaving me about an 8-iron distance to the middle of the green. I took the 6-iron out of the bag; caddy James Reynolds objected, saying that was too much club. I explained that with a 6-shot lead the only way I could possibly lose the championship would be hitting short and into the creek or a bunker.

My plan was to hit long, a little over the green where there were no bunkers. A large gallery was behind the green, but I knew I wouldn't be that far over. Had I been trailing, I would have attacked the hole despite the obvious risks.

Compromising with the caddy, I hit a 7-iron precisely as planned. I

Receiving congratulations from 1957 runnerup Bob Lowry, Jr., of Huntsville.

chipped on the green, stopping about three feet from the hole, sank the putt for my 69 and won my first state championship, which I had long worked for.

Now my name would go on the permanent state championship trophy with many of my role models: Sam Perry (four times champion), father and son Gordon Smith Jr., and Gordon III, Harry Pritchett, Scudday Horner, Jack Horner, Dr. A.B. "Buck" Harris, Bob Gregory and, way back in 1922, H.G. "Diddy" Seibels, the 1899 Sewanee football hero.

Friend and AGA President Tommy Nicol, speaking at the trophy presentation, was generous: "Elbert's win is long overdue . . . he has been knocking at the door a long time." And "his victory is unique because he is both player and administrator."

Maury Farrell, WAPI radio sports reporter, who had pioneered radio coverage back when I won the county championship, had covered the just-finished tournament. He motioned me aside and asked for some on-the-air comments and for the ball I had holed out with — a keepsake for his son. I was happy to oblige.

Along with the Sam Perry Trophy, I was presented a beautiful silver tray. The Perry Trophy would stay at my home club, Birmingham Country Club, for a year, longer if I could successfully defend the title.

1958

I ADMIT I BEGAN focusing early on the 1958 state tournament to be played at Mobile Country Club. I knew the odds were against me, or anyone else, winning consecutive state championships, but if I could successfully defend my title, it could never be said that I was not a good player.

Mobile Country Club has many similarities to Mountain Brook in that it demands straight driving and accurate iron play. It's another fine old course designed by Donald Ross.

Unlike at Mountain Brook, we had to play both the course and the weather. All four days we encountered both rain and wind, Gulf Coast squally weather. As a result, scoring was high.

I didn't play the first round like a defending champion. I shot a 77, which left me tied with five others for about 17th place.

The leaders were Jim Cotton of Montgomery 71; Billy Shelton of Anniston 73; Bob Lowry, Jr., of Huntsville, Bob Burch of Mobile and Johnny Gross, Jr., of Birmingham 74. Seven entrants shot 76s. And six of us, 77s.

But it's never been my nature to wring my hands or throw in the towel. By the end of another day of constant rain and changing winds, according to Grantland Rice, II, of *The Birmingham News*, I had improved to a 73, only a stroke back of leaders Gross and Burch.

Indicative of the troubles rain brought, Lowry had incurred a lost-ball penalty. Except for that penalty, he would have been the leader.

Had my treasured tutor, Sam Byrd, been with me, he probably would have counseled me "rely on your swing." I was in the running and determined to play my game, as Byrd had taught me.

With a second straight 1-over 73 Saturday, I moved into a two-stroke lead. Dick Pride of Tuscaloosa held second place at 225 after playing the last five holes, the toughest stretch, at 1-under. Lowry and Gilbert Wesley were tied at 226, followed by Tommy Nicol and Ed Brown at 227. Burch and Gross were 5 shots back of me.

Rice reported that I had had nine 1-putt greens and a string of 10 straight 4s from the seventh until I bogeyed the 18th.

Pride, 20-year-old University of Alabama student, slugged it out with me in the final round on Sunday. It was nip-and-tuck all the way after I took a

Relaxing after successfully defending my state title at Mobile Country Club, 1958.

near-disastrous 7 on the par-4 fourth hole. I had to shoot the "murderous" last four holes in par to finish with a 76 to go with my 77-73-73.

Pride had finished 75-77-73-74. He had bogeyed the 18th and gone inside to sweat out my finish. My drive at 18 landed in the rough, but, as Rice reported, I cracked a long iron but left it a little short of the green, pitched on and sank a four-footer for a par 4 that tied us at 299, a four-round average of 74.75 compared to my 287 and 71.75 average at Mountain Brook.

The sudden-death playoff began at the No. 1 tee. I won a coin toss to see who would hit first and chose to hit second so I could see what Pride did with his tee shot. He pushed it somewhat to the right on the par-4 hole.

As it had been raining and the rough had not been cut in several days, I knew he would not have an easy second shot. I decided to hit my 3-wood instead of the driver to be sure I was in the fairway. I did hit the fairway and hit my second shot into the middle of the green.

Dick hit a very fine shot out of the rough but a little too strong and it flew the green. His third shot was on the green and he two-putted for a 5. I two-putted for my par 4 to become the first golfer in 10 years to successfully defend my title.

Gillett Burton of Mobile was third at 303. Billy Shelton and John Gross of Birmingham tied for fourth at 304 and Bobby Burch of Mobile was sixth at 307.

Bob Phillips, AGA secretary-treasurer, had a yen for statistics. He wrote that my 72-hole effort was comprised of 10 birdies, 44 pars, 16 bogeys, 1 double bogey and 1 triple bogey. He calculated also that if Pride and I had been scored on four rounds of match play, I would have won 3 and 1.

After the trophy presentation I phoned Jess Ann, who with our year-old daughter Anne was visiting her parents in Huntsville, to tell her I had won. She was immensely pleased, of course, but told me she already had heard the news on radio. That shows you how big radio was in our lives back then.

Rather than drive back to Birmingham late, I stayed over and went out Monday morning to get the Mobile paper's report on my triumph. Would you believe: the newspaper plant had been hit by fire the evening before and there was no paper!

1959

AS A PART OF MY NEWSPAPER clippings in the Museum of the Alabama Sports Hall of Fame, an article is entitled, "Jemison Seeks Third Straight State Title."

The championship site was to be the Gadsden Country Club, where I had twice been a bridesmaid, in the 1949 Invitational Tournament and in the 1950 State Championship. I remember asking myself: Can I win in Gadsden? I knew that no one had ever won three consecutive championships. Now I was going to attempt the impossible.

My opening round was 73, followed by a 71 for 144, which placed me in a tie for the lead. I recall thinking that I just might pull off the impossible and win my third straight.

But that was not to be. I recall hitting the ball as well as I did in the first two rounds, but a self-imposed penalty shot occurred. On the third hole I was over the green in the rough. Having had little rain and without a sprinkler system, the grass was dry and brittle. I soled my wedge behind the ball; it moved and did not return to its original resting place, calling for a stroke penalty. That resulted in a 6 on a par-5 hole.

I reported to my fellow competitor, who had my scorecard, that I had scored 6 on the hole and explained the penalty shot. He said he had not seen the ball move and asked if I was certain the ball had not returned to its original resting place. I replied I was positive, so I incurred the penalty.

My third-round score was 75, so I lost ground to the leaders. I recall feeling that I was just not supposed to win a third straight tournament. My last round was 77 for a total of 296, which left me in 10th.

Art Gleason and Sonny Holt, both of Selma, were tied after 72 holes. Art

Jess Ann and Anne join me in admiring the Sam Perry Memorial State Championship Trophy on display at Birmingham Country Club.

won his first and only state tournament on the second extra hole of their playoff. Sonny had won the state in 1955 in Montgomery.

Walter Wood was third, Dick Spencer fourth, and Bob Lowry, Jr., fifth.

SEVERAL FINE 1950s PLAYERS I always considered capable never won the state, among them Jim Head, Bob Lowry, Jr., Tommy Nicol, Walter Wood, John Rogers and Frank Campbell. They were like the great Sam Snead who never won a U.S. Open.

As a postscript to my two state championships and the near-misses in 1950 and 1959, Jimmy Bryan of *The Birmingham News* asked me on the 30th anniversary of the second title, "Elbert, why don't you play the state this year, for old times' sake?"

I explained that nowadays I'm outdriven an average 40 yards a hole by the young crowd. With 14 driving holes and four rounds, that means I would be spotting the limberjacks about a mile advantage before we teed off in a tournament. That's one large why!

12
Either Too Young
or Too Old

S o, life begins at 40, it's said. Well, what of golf life — what happens at 40? If you were born in a year ending in 0 as I was, 1920, you probably are a little more aware than others as a decade runs out.

As 1960 came on, I looked ahead to Oct. 27 and birthday No. 40. I guess everybody takes inventory in that milestone year, as: What have I done and what's down the road?

Do golfers turning 40 wonder if they're nearing burnout? I didn't. At least, I don't recall that I did. I certainly didn't think I could still go toe-to-toe with the young turks. But I was still hitting the ball well, I could make a decent showing in exhibitions with visiting professionals, and I looked ahead to competing in Senior tournaments in a few years.

So just where was I as I neared 40? Three and a half decades later, looking back at that period, I know that I was in something I now can call "the in-between years." Too old to compete with the young, too young to compete with the old, the seniors.

THOSE IN-BETWEEN YEARS were among my most enjoyable. They also were among my most trying.

Some of us in golf's no-man's-land age-wise began to chafe at being left out, so the line about necessity being the mother of invention came into play.

We "invented" a division for us in-betweeners. We called it the Junior-Senior State Championship, to make it sound prestigious, and we convinced AGA Secretary Bob Phillips the Junior-Senior event should be played inside the annual AGA tournament.

Fine with him, Phillips said, but it will cost you Junior-Seniors an extra five dollars. "Got to help pay for the prizes," he explained. So we in-betweeners (ages 45 to 54) could still compete for the AGA championship, in theory anyway, but simultaneously we could compete for the Junior-Senior title, much more reachable.

The next year I proposed moving up the Junior-Senior age bracket to 46-54 and a year later to 47-54. MassMutual colleague and bench jockey Malcolm McDonald saw through that strategy, he claimed, pointing out that the low side of the age bracket went up a year as I got a year older. I denied his allegation that I was blocking out younger competitors, but I wasn't very convincing!

Although I will elaborate later about the administrative side of my golf years, it should be mentioned in this between-years recounting that in the 1960s, my involvement in administration took on new dimensions. What resulted was a see-saw development: As my competitive efforts diminished, my administrative involvement grew.

After serving on both the AGA and SGA boards since 1952, in 1954 I had been appointed to the USGA Sectional Affairs Committee and in 1970 I went on the USGA Executive Committee, the 16-member governing body of American golf.

MEANWHILE, IN THOSE IN-BETWEEN YEARS I met and played with some of the truly big names in golf; I say that not in boast but in salute to people who helped to elevate golf.

Before I recount the exhibitions that brought more pro golf stars to Birmingham, I must detour.

In the 1960s decade my golf encountered some bumps in the road, primarily health problems. In 1962 I suffered a severe appendix rupture and peritonitis. I was in Carraway Methodist Hospital about three weeks and lost more than 30 pounds. Some of the weight loss was muscle mass, which was apparent when I returned to golf.

A great friend, golf partner and superb surgeon, Dr. William C. Tucker, moved into Carraway, slept there during my critical days and got me out of the woods.

In 1968 I had recurring gall bladder trouble and eventually had surgery. Again Dr. Tucker took excellent care of me during an eight-day hospital stay. The lengthy stay contrasts with today's two-day stay that laser surgery makes possible.

State Tournament planners (left to right): Joe King, Hollis Geiger, Jemison and Bob Phillips.

After each of the hospital visits, I was, understandably, quite a while getting back into full golf swing.

IN 1960 AND 1961, ARNOLD PALMER, everybody's golf idol, came to Birmingham for charity exhibitions sponsored by the Sertoma Club.

The 1960 event, played in October at Birmingham Country Club, drew about 2,500 fans despite rain and cold. Arnie and I were paired against Paddy LaClair and Buddy DeBardeleben.

Still in his prime years (he won the U.S. Open later that year) and golf's top drawing card, Palmer was cheered on by the Birmingham division of his fan "army" and he didn't disappoint. He shot a crowd-pleasing 68, three under par. We were strung out behind: LaClair 73, Jemison 79 and DeBardeleben 81. Palmer/Jemison won 3 and 1.

Naturally we hometowners wanted to play our best but what we shot was not top priority — most eyes were on the star, magnificent Arnold Palmer, America's most-loved golfer; indeed, most-loved athlete.

Arnie could do no wrong, that day or any other. A few weeks prior to his Birmingham appearance, he had made a horrendous 12, seven over par, in the

Enrolling Don Meredith and Paul Bryant in USGA Members Program.

Los Angeles Open. When a reporter asked how could he, Arnold Palmer, make a 12 on that hole, he said the answer was obvious: because he had missed a putt on his 11th stroke. Was he forever ruined? Hardly; he won the next two pro tournaments.

Speaking of putts, in that exhibition as in others, short putts often were given — except when a cry rang out from the gallery, "Make him putt it!" We knew what that meant; wagers had been made.

When we had finished that wet, cold round at the Country Club, I told the golfers and wives (Arnie's Winnie was with him), "We'll meet at my house." Word spread that the Palmers would be at the Jemisons' and by the time we drove there our driveway was full.

Arnie quickly made his wishes known: "Let's don't go out to eat." We sent for beverages and built a fire. Arnie was not the sit-back-and-be-waited-on type; he checked to see what snacks were available, found wieners and put them on to boil. Somebody else reached for the peanut butter jar, another found cheese and pretty soon the pantry was almost bare and the kitchen looked like a storm had passed through.

We didn't have to suggest that our visitors relax. Most of them took off their shoes and warmed their stockinged feet at the fireplace. Winnie and Arnie had two young daughters at home and our Anne was 4, so Winnie, Jess Ann and the other women shared girl talk.

I couldn't list all our guests that evening, but among them were Charley and Kitty Boswell and Hall Thompson, along with numerous good golfing friends who had been in the gallery that day. Arnie relaxed by the fire with our Anne in his lap. Someone took their picture and for almost 40 years that photo has helped us relive an occasion we will never forget.

Palmer returned in 1961 for another Sertoma benefit exhibition, and that time the weather cooperated, making a grand event even grander. Arnie was the guest of Sertoma President J.V. Rives and Mrs. Rives. In the golf exhibition, Palmer and host pro Jim Dunkerly were surprised by amateurs David Boyd of Atlanta and Bobby McClung of Birmingham. I had suggested that David play in my stead because he had won the last two Birmingham Invitationals and deserved the attention.

Palmer and Boyd shared rounds of 77, but the amateurs won 3 and 2 and Arnie apologized. "I don't know when I've played so poorly," he told the Birmingham division of his army. The admiration factor was not affected.

I now have had the honor and pleasure of knowing Arnold Palmer, golf's

A gathering at our home after a Palmer exhibition. Anne Jemison is in Arnold's lap next to Charley Boswell;
'n back, Kitty Boswell, Winnie Palmer, Margaret DeBardeleben and Jess Ann.

Golf legend Gene Sarazen and Joe King become USGA Members.

greatest ambassador, since 1954. After 22 years, we continue to serve together on the United States Golf Association Members Committee.

Palmer is a dedicated, competitive warm-hearted and caring human being. A favorite with people the world over, he is a fun and jovial golf partner.

I REGAINED SOME of my competitive edge in 1964 by winning the Birmingham Country Club club tournament. I had won it once before, in 1952.

Tour pro Juan "Chi Chi" Rodriguez, an all-time gallery favorite, and Ed Nelson, Dr. Rossi of television's Peyton Place, played an exhibition at Birmingham's Green Valley Club in 1965. The Birmingham Golf Association, comprised of clubs in the Jefferson County area, brought the stars to Birmingham to help raise funds for the BGA's junior golfers fund. Club pro Bob Ledbetter and I rounded out the foursome.

Chi Chi, entertaining the gallery between shots, had a one-under par 71, Ledbetter 74, Jemison 76 and Nelson was "somewhere in the 90s." Ledbetter and I won 2 and 1 in a match close all the way. The large gallery expressed appreciation for some good golf and a lot of laughs, along with a successful fund-raising for junior golf.

Despite the fact that in those years exhibition guest stars did not charge a fee, only travel and lodging expenses, once in a while good intentions got out of hand. They did in 1967 when we brought in a bunch of headliners including Jack Nicklaus, Mason Rudolph, Doug Sanders, and composer Hoagy Carmichael.

The promoter for the BGA had simply gotten in over his head and when we compared what we had raised against what we had spent, we were $6,000 in the hole. We took our dilemma to banker Norman Pless, who agreed to lend us the $6,000 if each of six applicants would agree to be responsible for the entire $6,000.

We proposed that each loan co-maker be responsible for $1,000, but it took us a while to convince Pless.

The next year we were back with more stars: Entertainer Dinah Shore, Ed Nelson in a repeat appearance, movie star Dale Robertson, pros Billy Casper, Bobby Nichols, Julius Boros and Frank Beard, plus Paul "Bear" Bryant, Chuck Jones and others.

Before teeing off at Birmingham Country Club, golf great Byron Nelson instructs Grantland Rice, III. Tuning 'n are Anne Jemison, Sidney Quarles and Tommy Luckie.

Paired for the exhibition at Birmingham Country Club: Ed Pascoe and Ralph Smallman, III, versus Jemison and Byron Nelson.

Because we had to pay only travel and lodging, we were able to pay off the previous year's bills and show a profit for the BGA junior program.

That night at our dinner/dance, Dinah Shore joshed me about not having danced with her. I explained that I had not recovered fully after surgery. She said we would wait for "a slow tune." So we waited and I got through the dance without trouble.

In 1968 I finally had the privilege of playing alongside Byron Nelson, in my view the greatest golfer of all time. Nelson was on his way to the Masters Tournament and agreed to stop over to play a benefit at the Birmingham Country Club. He and I teamed to defeat two good golfers, Ed Pascoe and Ralph Smallman III 1-up.

Jemison, Buddy DeBardeleben, Palmer and Paddy LaClair before teeing off in exhibition.

A valued friend for almost 50 years, Nelson would come to Birmingham some 15 years later for my induction into the Alabama Sports Hall of Fame. Byron personifies all that is great and good about the game of golf. He is loyal to his friends and enjoys doing things for others less fortunate.

It has always been a thrill for me to tee off with perhaps the greatest golfer of them all.

Meanwhile, my relationship with blind golf champion Charley Boswell grew more involved. The Birmingham Golf Association that by now had considerable experience in conducting exhibitions set up a committee to help Boswell with his Charley Boswell Celebrity Classic that would raise more than a million dollars for the Eye Foundation Hospital.

Let me here mention the name of "Little Bill" Ireland, who was most helpful with the Boswell Classic. What a shame that "Little Bill" had been badly injured in a late-1940s automobile accident that curtailed a promising competitive golf career. I remember him well before World War II as an outstanding young player.

Other lasting friends whose names come to mind: Jack Blackwell, Bob Yoe

Light moment at Birmingham Golf Association exhibition. Next to me, Miss Birmingham Golf Association, then Ed Nelson (Dr. Rossi of TV's Peyton Place) and golf tour favorite Chi Chi Rodriguez.

and Jack Shannon, among many others.

The in-between years were among my most enjoyable, but I confess I was eager to get back into spirited competition. That would come with Senior golf.

13
Senior Golf Citizen

Author Oliver Goldsmith said he loved everything old: old friends, old times, old manners, old books, old wines. Senior golfers can relate. But if the young crowd thinks we've been put out to pasture, they're wrong. In many ways, golf's golden years are the best, for which our earlier years prepared us.

Is the man in his dotage, you may wonder, and my resounding response is: Hear me out.

Having recorded my best (a.k.a. my younger) golf years and then my in-between times, I look now at my Senior years, which continue even yet but in much-subdued fashion.

Perhaps surprising to golfer-readers approaching 55: I earnestly believe that some of your most rewarding golf lies ahead.

CONTRARY TO WORRYING about being put out to pasture, I actually looked forward to competing in the Seniors ranks.

Of course, I would have liked to continue being an outside possibility to win a third state championship and various other tournaments I had won, but reality sets in and you set your sights on new goals.

Turning 55 in 1975, I willingly, enthusiastically accepted the invitation to become a member of the Alabama Seniors Golf Association, aware that I

Among participants in charity exhibition at Pine Tree Country Club, Birmingham, in 1978 (left to right): Joe King, Dick Ford of Grand Rapids, Mich., in back, Judy Kimball, Jemison, Bo Russell in back, former President Gerald R. Ford, John Forney in back, Jerry Siegel, Jim Martin in back, Hollis Stacy, Arnold Palmer, Coach Paul Bryant and Dr. David Mathews, then University of Alabama president.

would still be matching shots with many of the people I had competed against in what I call regular golf among fellow Alabamians. They included old-friend golfers like Joe King, Dr. Brooks Cotten, Allyn Thames, Weldon Doe, Buddy Smith, Gene Moor, Walter Wood, Buddy DeBardeleben, Jackie Cummings and two longtime close friends, now deceased, Buddy Walker and Tommy Nicol, both of Tuscaloosa.

Now I was a rookie again, a Senior rookie, of course, and in 1976 and 1977 State Senior Tournaments I was able to match my back-to-back State amateur championships of 1957 and '58.

Playing at Birmingham Country Club in 1976, my first time to enter the state Senior, I won with a three-round 225 for an average 75 per round. M.G. Walker was second with 226 and boyhood friend Brooks Cotten was third with 227.

The next year at the Anniston Country Club I successfully defended the Alabama Senior title with a three-round total of 223, a 74.3 average. Joe King, my longtime close friend, fellow competitor and golf administrator, was second with 224. M.G. Walker was third with 228.

I qualified for a shot at the Senior National Amateur championship in 1977 at Peabody, Mass., and for the U.S. Senior championship in 1980 at Salem, Mass. Allow me to sidetrack briefly for a railroad note.

Proof positive that not all good golfers wear gray flannel suits, labor in insurances offices as I do or in other white-collar jobs: On that 1980 trip to the U.S. Senior, my roommate was a railroad engineer, Bob Winters of Birmingham. The other two sectional qualifiers from our area were Joe King and Bancroft Timmons.

As Winters' roommate I became accustomed to waking up a little earlier than customary. Because of his railroad job, I presume, he would wake up at 4 and reach for the telephone to call his wife in Birmingham. His opening line probably was old hat to her: "You ought to be out feeding the chickens!"

Other than rising early (after snoring heavily most of the night) Bob was a congenial roommate. One night a noreaster (windy, rainy storm, y'all) came through, bringing shivery weather. Winters looked out, saw a Sears store across the street and had a remedy. "Let's go get some long-johns." We did.

In later years, Winters would help co-found the Birmingham Regional Association of Golfing Seniors. He suggested using the acronym BRAG. We need more golfers like Bob Winters.

By the way, I had a valid excuse for not making the cut at that tournament. When I had first mentioned going to Massachusetts for the U.S. Senior, Jess Ann had reminded me her family, the Yarbroughs, were having a reunion in Huntsville that weekend. By playing negatively and missing the cut by two strokes, I made it to the reunion. Conscience penalty, I guess.

For the record, in addition to the two back-to-back State Seniors championships, the books show that I won Country Club of Birmingham Seniors championships in 1979 and 1982 and Mountain Brook Club (Birmingham) championships in 1983, 1984, 1987 and was co-winner in 1988, with Dr. Wood Herren, who has also been a fine tennis player and a close friend since boyhood days.

The Mountain Brook Club, which did not have a permanent trophy for its Senior champion, decided to establish one and because I had won the tournament several times, to name the trophy for me. My brother-in-law, Dr.

Byron Nelson accepts a plaque expressing appreciation for his participation as an honorary competitor in the 1987 Mountain Brook Club Senior Tournament.

George W. "Buzz" Matthews, Jr., as chairman of the club's "bowl" committee, informed me of the decision and I told him I was deeply honored.

Then "the Great One," as I know him, dropped the other shoe. "And we thought perhaps the Jemisons would like to help defray costs of the trophy." So, as the world turns, that's how my name is listed with other winners on the trophy bearing my name!

Now let me salute Alabama's two finest-ever Senior golfers: Huntsville's Frank Campbell, who won an unbelievable nine straight Alabama Senior championships, and Tuscaloosa's Jackie Cummings, who won the 1990 National Senior championship, played at the Desert Forest Country Club in Carefree, Ariz., and three Alabama amateur championships. Both good friends, both great champions.

UNTIL SENIOR COMPETITION took root and became widespread nationally, regionally and locally, golfers were considered more or less over the hill when they turned 55 or 60. But consider just one current f'r-instance, Birmingham's yearly Bruno's Senior pro tournament. Large numbers of name players compete and post impressive rounds to the applause of large galleries.

The Birmingham club senior tournaments, the Alabama Senior tournament and the National Senior attract large entry lists. Galleries are modest compared to regular tournaments, but there are rewards for participants.

Senior golf is highly competitive, but not as intense as was, say, the Birmingham Invitational or the Alabama Amateur. Television golf has led to smaller galleries, but the fans who do turn out are enthusiastic and supportive. Much of the intense competitive spirit of regular golf has carried over into Senior events. You still want very much to win; that never changes. But despite keen competition, the overall atmosphere is more relaxed. Most Seniors are thoroughly familiar with the rules, with the equipment they're comfortable with, and their limitations (such as losing a yard or so a year on your drives). So you can play your best and still have a lot of fun.

A marked difference, one I noted immediately upon becoming a Senior, is the flair of fellowship. The better players still want to win, but it's obvious that many golfers play on the Senior level for the fellowship. There are more parties, more dinners, more cocktails.

I would say the Alabama Senior Golf Association is about 50 percent social. At one Alabama Senior Tournament, played at Jekyll Island, Ga., we had 156 players and 153 wives.

In conjunction with the Senior men's tournament, arrangements are made for wives to play two days at another course. It's keen competition but largely a fun event.

We have about 500 members in the Alabama Seniors Golf Association, usually playing four tournaments a year. The affairs of the association are determined by its Board of Governors and ably implemented by Van Carlisle, the secretary-treasurer, and his superb assistant, Judy Carlisle, who has made noteworthy contributions to the Alabama Seniors Golf Association and to the Legendary Seniors Amateur Classic.

Mrs. John (Jean) McCarley, wife of a retired internist, has been perennial golf chairwoman, dedicated and seemingly tireless.

Two other Senior golf associations of which I am privileged to be a member are the Southern Seniors and the U.S. Seniors.

My participation in the administrative side of golf continued through the several offices I held in Senior organizations, covered next in the chapter on administration.

Essential Checkpoints of the Golf Swing

Compiled by Elbert S. Jemison, Jr.

These checkpoints may not be totally agreed upon by all teachers and good golfers. They were compiled from personal instructors, from observing great golfers and from numerous instructional articles that I applied while playing.

1 — The hands (grip) should work as a team.

2 — The speed of the hands should be the same throughout the swing.

3 — At address, there should be a substantially straight line from the left shoulder to the hands and to the clubhead.

4 — At address, the arms are extended (not stiff) with the right arm slightly lower than the left.

5 — The width of the feet apart should be approximately the width of the shoulders.

6 — At address, for the longer clubs, the ball should be on line just inside the left heel; toward the center for shorter clubs.

7 — For the right-handed player, the left side predominates the swing. It is the control and directional side.

8 — At the beginning of the swing (set in motion by the left side) the clubhead should take a path directly behind the ball.

9 — At the top of the back swing, the weight should be substantially on the right heel.

10 — The golf swing is a continuous movement (no complete stopping at the top of the back swing). As Percy Boomer, the great English teacher, describes it in his book *On Learning Golf*: "waiting in motion."

11 — The reverse action starts prior to reaching the top of the back swing by returning the left heel to the ground, which triggers the downward action. (As the great teacher Harvey Pennick wrote in his *Little Red Book*: "If there is any such thing as a magic move in the golf swing, it is to start your downswing letting your weight shift to your left foot while bringing your right elbow back down to your body. This is one move, not two."

12 — One should feel that the maximum clubhead speed is approximately eight inches past where the ball was resting in place.

13 — Throughout the swing the last two fingers of the left hand should be more firmly on the grip than the other fingers.

14 — Harvie Ward, the fine player and teacher, said "attack the ball from the rear" to help cure the problem of hitting from the top (of the swing).

15 — After impact of the clubhead with the ball, the eyes and head should follow the shot.

16 — Brace against the right leg on the backswing.

17 — "It's almost impossible to stand too close to the ball at address" — Byron Nelson.

18 — One should not try to hit the ball; instead, create the proper golf swing that will cause the ball to go on the intended flight and direction.

19 — Never let the putter head get ahead of the hands until after contact with the ball.

I purposely listed 19 checkpoints so that the next time you play 18 holes you will have one point per hole on which to concentrate, plus having one to discuss at the 19th hole with a beverage. But, remember, the best instruction is obtained from your professional.

14
Administering the Game

The responsibilities of a golf administrator, which I was for 50 years, can be as routine as overseeing a club junior tournament, as hush-hush as secretly testing a 1.66-inch U.S.-British compromise-size golf ball, as suspenseful as handling a death threat against Hubert Green in a U.S. Open.

In those 50 years, I moved from token administration all the way to election to the United States Golf Association Executive Committee for eight years of service on this governing body of American golf. Service on that committee included meetings with the Royal and Ancient Golf Club at St. Andrews, Scotland.

The Hubert Green episode, which played out in 1977 at Tulsa's Southern Hills Golf Club, is one of my most memorable, probably because I had a direct role in it.

Despite having won impressively on the PGA tour, Birmingham's Hubert Green had yet to win a major title. The one he was chasing in 1977 was the most coveted of all. After 14 holes of the final Open round, he was leading by a stroke.

The FBI office in Oklahoma City had gotten a phone call that day from a woman who said three men were on their way "to shoot Hubert Green on the 15th green."

Crank call or not, the threat had to be handled. By the time the Management Committee, of which as USGA secretary I was a member, got word of the death threat, Green was playing the 10th hole.

The Management Committee, comprised of the officers empowered by the USGA to act in just such emergency circumstances, huddled immediately. We decided these options were available to relay to Hubert:

1. Presume the threat was a crank call and do nothing.
2. Suspend play long enough to increase security.
3. For complete safety, accept Hubert's withdrawal.

FRANK D. "SANDY" TATUM, USGA vice president and chairman of the Championship Committee, asked me to be the one to tell Hubert of the death threat "because you're both from Birmingham and you know him best."

So, after Hubert completed the 14th hole, we approached him. I quietly told him of the threat and what we felt his options were. Whatever he may have felt, he said simply that he would continue playing, that if he withdrew the cranks would use threats to stop other sports events.

Hubert appeared calm and unshaken. His playing partners and the large gallery were unaware of the threat, which, as almost all do, proved to be a crank call.

With Lou Graham breathing down his neck, Hubert sank a short pressure putt on the 18th to win the Open by a stroke and claim his first major championship. He had said he needed to win a major to establish himself as a great player, and now he had.

What a triumph! For Hubert Green, for his supporters, for golf generally. And, I told myself, in a small way for our Management Committee.

IN THE MID-1970s I participated in another administrative action that also was undercover but was totally different from the Green drama.

Golfers and fans alike know that Americans didn't begin to take golf seriously until early in the 20th century, but once bitten, they almost took over the game the Scots had begun centuries earlier.

The two leading golf organizations, the Royal and Ancient Golf Club of St. Andrews, Scotland, and the United States Golf Association, agreed on common rules and equipment specifications — with one exception, ball size.

The British used a ball 1.62 inches in diameter, the Americans used one measuring 1.68. With their smaller ball, British golfers could play better in their island's strong winds.

Through the years, U.S.-British compromise efforts on ball size increased. In the 1970s the USGA and R and A sought compromise on a world-wide ball that would be the same weight, size and velocity, possibly 1.66 inches in diameter.

As a member of the USGA Executive Committee, along with several other American golfers, I began testing the 1.66 ball, hitting all by myself at Mountain Brook Club's 10th hole, where there was almost no chance of losing a ball.

My findings were that I preferred our 1.68 ball; however, I felt strongly that we needed a common-size ball for worldwide uniformity. If the R and A found the 1.66 experimental ball favorable, I thought the USGA should agree.

Word leaked out about our testing. American golfers, amateur and professional, made it clear they preferred to keep the 1.68 ball. Then came a surprise break: the R and A advised us they would accept our 1.68 to be the worldwide ball!

I felt then and still feel that the R and A had made a major concession for the good of the game. After all, they had used the 1.62 ball a long, long time.

LOOKING BACK AT A LIFETIME in golf, I marvel at the changes that my being in administration have brought in my career. I think without question that my role as a golf official played a major part in my being inducted into the Alabama Sports Hall of Fame. Also, because of that role I have met a host of entertainment and sports stars, have developed a warm friendship with a U.S. President and have made lasting friendships with golfers and golf administrators in America and other countries.

And yet, it all happened almost by accident. At the outset I got into administration out of necessity. For example, it was necessity when I helped put together golf teams at Ramsay High School, Sewanee Military Academy, assisted with team affairs at the University of Virginia and, after World War II, at the University of Alabama.

After that, nature took its course: the urge to play, the need to promote and manage. Each move seemed to move me toward the next until one day I reached the ultimate when elected to the Executive Committee of the United States Golf Association.

Saying it happened by accident is not totally accurate. I think much of what propelled me toward being a golf administrator was ingrained, was there all the time. I have guessed that no more than 5 percent of those who play golf are interested in or inclined toward administration; from the first I was in that 5 percent.

Perhaps my early leaning toward the military will help explain. I preferred organization, authority, leadership, action. And I relished interaction with people.

At Ramsay High I saw the possibility of forming a golf team and went right to work on it. The circumstances were the same at SMA and three years later when I assisted a team at the University of Virginia. When World War II ended in Europe, I readily accepted the order to form a 3rd Army golf team that was supposed to play other service teams. That didn't materialize because of an order to return to the United States.

After leaving the University of Alabama, I entered another level of administration by arranging and playing in professional-amateur exhibitions with encouragement from my company, MassMutual, to benefit worthy charities in the Birmingham area. That led to assisting with tournaments and to election to club offices and full-scale involvement in golf administration at several levels. For reader convenience, I will summarize.

CLUBS

Country club presidents usually rise to that office by having served several years as directors and usually doing major committee work such as being golf chairman. I became Birmingham Country Club president in 1961, one of the youngest ever in that office. Previously I had been tournament chairman, golf chairman, director, and vice president.

While I was president we completely remodeled the West Course with Robert Trent Jones, the renowned architect. We also built the West Lounge for about $278,000, much less than was spent later on the East Room.

At Mountain Brook Club I was golf chairman, vice president, then president in 1978. I served on the BCC board 17 years and on the Mountain Brook board 12 years. I came back as finance chairman at both clubs after being president. I was on the Mountain Brook committee that oversaw remodeling of the golf course with John LaFoy as architect.

BIRMINGHAM GOLF ASSOCIATION

The Vestavia Country Club once held an annual event called Champions Night Dinner. One year at this dinner someone suggested that establishing a Birmingham Golf Association would enable all member clubs to pool their manpower to assist with exhibitions, rules seminars, junior golf and materials buying power.

The suggestion became reality in 1964, thanks in large part to the influence and participation of people such as Jim Head, Jr., L.J. Griffis, Bob Ramsay, Johnny Thames, Jerry Seigel, "Little Bill" Ireland, Walter Wood and Bancroft Timmons.

The association blossomed as hoped and soon was sponsoring pro-am exhibitions, described in an earlier chapter, to raise funds for junior golf and Birmingham charities. I assisted in the promotion of and played in the exhibition and was rewarded when the BGA established the Elbert S. Jemison, Jr., Permanent Junior Trophy. I was and am deeply honored.

The BGA also assisted the Birmingham Ladies Golf Association, formed about 1970 with Ann Samford Upchurch as driving-force founder.

With advent of the Charley Boswell Celebrity Golf Classic in 1974, the BGA-sponsored exhibitions and the Birmingham LPGA-sponsored events ended. For 15 years BGA member clubs assisted with the Boswell event, which raised more than a million dollars for the Eye Foundation Hospital.

Longtime administrator Jim Spader did a fine job keeping BGA clubs and members enthusiastic about the Boswell classic. In 1965 the Birmingham Golf Association Hall of Fame was established with Sam Perry, Bill McWane, Charley Boswell and Elbert S. Jemison, Jr., as charter members. It was a signal honor for the four of us. I was in august company.

ALABAMA GOLF ASSOCIATION

It's hard for me to think of the Alabama Golf Association without thinking of Bob Phillips, longtime secretary-treasurer. As many of you will remember, Bob was a stickler on rules, yet he seemed to operate the AGA out of his back pocket.

I remember once as we drove to a tournament in Selma, we were talking about the case of a young amateur golfer who had won a new car in a hole-in-one contest but had lost his amateur status because of the car.

I asked, "Bob, what would you do if you won a new car that way?" I knew how he insisted that amateurs stay simon-pure.

"Are you kidding?" he said, laughing. "I'd take the car."

"But . . . " I started to protest.

"Who cares if I'm not an amateur," he said, and that was that.

The longtime sports editor of the old *Birmingham Age-Herald* and later executive sports editor of the *Post-Herald* helped hold the AGA together. He was our friend and staunch supporter. He told me once that we had traveled together to 25 out-of-town state championships.

As our permanent secretary-treasurer, he was not very formal when, at board meetings, he was asked for a financial report. "Oh, we're in good shape," he would say. "Don't worry about it."

We never gave him a paycheck, just something we called honorariums. That's the way he wanted it.

WHEN I JOINED the AGA board in 1951 I continued entering the state championship tournament. That meant that when I teed off, I took off my administrative hat. You can't officiate your own play.

Putting on the state tournament and the state junior tournament was the main function of the state association. For me the chief rewards were the friendships that developed with others interested in administration, golfers like Joe King, Allyn Thames, Bobby Graves, Tommy Nicol, Harry Pritchett, Byron Bower, Gordon Smith, Jr., Homer "Jug" Knight, Bob Lowry and Phillip Moss, and many others.

I was on the Alabama association board 30 years, was twice its president and now am a director emeritus.

SOUTHERN GOLF ASSOCIATION

Overlapping many of my years with the AGA, I served 30 years as a Southern Golf Association director, was president a year and am a director emeritus. I was elected to the SGA board in 1953. The SGA, whose member states stretch from Virginia to Texas, serves 14 states.

Most of the SGA's attention is directed toward the annual Southern tournament. In that connection, because I was a frequent competitor, I believe I was helpful in choosing sites for the tournament because I knew what type courses the entrants liked.

Another contribution I made to the SGA tournament: I knew the better players around the South and I urged as many as possible to enter the tournaments. That helped to elevate the level of competition.

USGA EXECUTIVE COMMITTEE

The United States Golf Association Executive Committee, comprised of 16 members, is the governing body of American golf. In joint deliberations with the Royal and Ancient Golf Club of Scotland, it enables golfers over the world to play under uniform rules.

The USGA is comprised of member clubs, not individuals. As of late 1996, of 8,827 member clubs and related facilities, 133 were in Alabama.

The USGA conducts 13 major national tournaments: Men's Open, Women's Open, Senior Open, National Amateur, National Women's Amateur, Amateur Public Links, Women's Amateur Public Links, Junior Amateur, Girls Junior Amateur, Mid-Amateur, Women's Mid-Amateur, Senior Amateur and Women's Senior Amateur.

On the international level the USGA conducts the Walker Cup (U.S. amateurs vs. England and Ireland) and the Curtis Cup, sometimes called the Women's Walker because it is the women's version of the Walker Cup matches.

Among aspects with which the USGA concerns itself: Rules and equipment, amateur status, the 13 major tournaments, the Members (formerly Associates) Program, the Handicap System (making possible fair competition for all golfers), turf research and overall protection and preservation of the integrity of the game.

To insure itself seasoned leadership, the USGA Executive Committee requires that some new members have served on boards in state or sectional associations. In my case, in 1970 I was director and past president of both the Alabama and Southern Golf Associations.

Arnold Palmer and I talk golf with President Ford in the Oval Office.

USGA Executive Committee members, who comprise the USGA Board of Directors, are on about a 72-hours notice for meetings and serve without pay; only the staff are paid.

IN MY EIGHT YEARS on the USGA Executive Committee I served in several capacities: helping officiate national championships, chairing the Amateur Status Committee, chairing the Green Section Committee, being on the Rules Committee two years, serving as both secretary and treasurer of the USGA, and serving on the committee that met in joint session with the Royal and Ancient Golf Club Committee in Scotland.

My chief contribution was helping institute the Associates (now

Members) Program that shored up USGA finances and enabled golfers, by enrolling, to become involved with the USGA. For that program I enlisted the support of President Ford and Arnold Palmer.

USGA treasurers before me had sought ways to make the USGA stronger financially. When I became treasurer, I outlined a plan to fellow members whereby golfers would contribute a specified fee to become a USGA Associate. The Associate would receive a Rules of Golf book, a subscription to the USGA Journal, information about the USGA, an Associates bag decal, an identification card and the satisfaction of supporting golf's governing body.

I decided to seek top-level help for the Associates program: First I asked Arnold Palmer to be honorary national chairman and he accepted. Then I wrote President Ford, asking that he sign on as first Associate. The President invited Palmer and me, along with my fellow officers, to the White House, where he enthusiastically helped launch the Associates.

The first year we enrolled 28,000 members; by the end of this decade we hope to have a million or more. Now called Members, the program provides substantial funds for the betterment of golf in America.

Later we asked President Ford for his assistance on a USGA request for tax deduction on funds spent promoting amateur golf. We told him we were spending our own money promoting our game. Our request to the IRS had been bogged down, but the President said he could help. In three weeks we had a favorable ruling.

Our visit to the Oval Office had been cordial and successful. To cap it off, the President asked us to make a return visit and to bring our wives, which we did.

As chairman of the USGA's Green Section, concerned with preserving top-quality turf for golf, I worked with our eight agronomists, who visited golf courses around the country. During the gasoline supply crisis, I once said in mock seriousness that I would provide mules for them to ride during the crisis. Some of them seemed to think I meant it!

The USGA's Amateur Status Committee is one of its busiest, deciding whether certain amateurs have stayed within the rules, as when accepting nonconforming prizes, and whether former non-amateurs are eligible for reinstatement. While I was chairman, hundreds of cases had to be considered by the committee.

Relaxed moment with President Ford and Arnold Palmer during a press conference at Pine Tree Country Club in 1978. They were in Birmingham for an exhibition golf match.

I was principal author of the language that comprises USGA policy on gambling. The underlying principle of that policy is to make clear that one does not play the game for remuneration but for love and enjoyment of the game. I am pleased that the language agreed on during my chairmanship of the committee remains intact.

I continue my service to the USGA as a member of the Members Committee and in any other way I can.

In 1975 I was on the USGA committee that went to St. Andrews, Scotland to confer with our British counterparts at the Royal and Ancient Golf Club. That was a rewarding experience, indeed, which I will recount in the next chapter.

15
Back to Where it all Began

No matter the locale — Copenhagen, Coventry, Capetown or Columbus — golf is played by the same rules. The global uniformity is possible thanks to two organizations, the United States Golf Association and the Royal and Ancient Golf Club of St. Andrews, Scotland.

In a nutshell: The USGA Executive Committee and the R and A meet every four years to confer on anything concerning golf, but principally rules, amateur status and equipment. What makes the meetings successful is the preparatory communication that sets the stage for the joint meetings.

When you are elected to the USGA's 16-member Executive Committee, as I was in 1970, you sit in judgment on American golf, as explained in the previous chapter. You also prepare for and attend the joint USGA - R and A meetings, also attended by French, German, Swedish and Spanish federation representatives.

Having served on the Executive Committee eight years, I participated in such a joint meeting in conjunction with the 1975 Walker Cup matches played on the Old Course at St. Andrews.

I had been in Scotland once before, in 1944, when the U.S. 35th Division landed at Glasgow, then moved on to southern England to prepare for departure to the ground war across the English Channel.

Three decades later I went back on a mission for golf. Wife Jess Ann and

18-year-old daughter Anne went along as did other wives, sons and daughters of Executive Committee members. We paid our own way, of course.

Our party was in a larger party. Following tradition, the Executive Committee was traveling with the 1975 U.S. Walker Cup team on its way to St. Andrews to play Britain's top amateurs. On the team were nonplaying captain Dr. Ed Updegraf and team members who included Jerry Pate (U of A), Curtis Strange, Jay Haas, Andy Bean and Craig Stadler. The daughters understandably were delighted to be in such company.

Any golfer with a sense of the game's history and tradition will understand what we felt as we arrived in the land where golf had begun hundreds of years ago. And our feelings were intensified when we set foot on the actual playing turf. Add the unmatched British hospitality and you have a dream trip.

Jess Ann's and Anne's host picked them up each day and drove them to luncheons, to teas, on sightseeing trips, to gardens and castles and other destinations, as did the other women's hosts, so it was a thoroughly rewarding occasion for them.

AFTER WORLD WAR II, golf in general had boomed as had international play, due in large part to convenient jet-age travel. Before the war the comparatively few Americans who played in the British Amateur and the British Open used the smaller (1.62 in. diameter) British ball. In turn, when Britons played in U.S. tournaments, they used the larger (1.68) American ball.

Ball-size and other differences in golf around the world convinced the USGA and the R and A, each of which wrote the rules for about 60 countries, that uniform rules and equipment were needed for worldwide uniformity. So the two governing bodies arranged for the joint meetings every four years.

What almost guaranteed the joint meeting's success was the spadework done by committee counterparts before the joint meeting. In 1975 I chaired the USGA's Amateur Status Committee. My counterpart, five-times British amateur champion Michael Bonallack, and I had corresponded many times on points likely to come up, so by meeting time we were ready. In later years Bonallack became secretary of the R and A. We still correspond.

A case that had come up back in the States was of special interest to me because it concerned Lee Mackey, Jr., of Birmingham. Mackey, you will remember, had gotten the golf world's attention in 1951 when he shot a record opening-round 64 in the U.S. Open at Philadelphia's Merion Golf Club. After 29 years as a professional, he now sought reinstatement as an amateur, presumably because he wanted to play in senior amateur events.

The key question was how much jail time (waiting) Mackey should serve before reinstatement. The committee agreed on my recommendation, which in the Mackey case was two years.

The various USGA and R and A committee chairmen — on rules, amateur status, implements and ball, etc. —

Posing (front row, right) with the joint American-British Amateur Status Committe at the Royal and Ancient Golf Club, St. Andrews, Scotland. (Photo by Ian Joy, St. Andrews)

met in separate rooms Tuesday, Wednesday and Thursday mornings, attended to business and quickly got to know each other on a first-name basis. In the afternoons those of us who were good enough played practice rounds with the Walker Cup team members on the Old Course. All four courses are wide open with almost no trees but with many hidden bunkers and other challenges. They are on the North Sea and almost always windy.

One day our Walker captain, Ed Updegraf, came to me asking a favor. He said the players were staying out too late with committeemen's daughters; he needed a curfew. We agreed on 10 p.m. — still daylight in Scotland! — and that solved his problem.

Another "problem" concerned Craig Stadler. Some of the daughters had conned a maid into letting them into Craig's room while he was busy at golf.

Anticipating that he would return to his room after his practice round, they greased the toilet seat in his bathroom.

Sure enough, Craig at first didn't notice the grease and almost took a bad spill. Captain Updegraf didn't think the prank was funny because, he said, Craig might have been hurt. But Craig took the prank in good humor, thinking his teammates were guilty. Later he learned that Anne Jemison and her friends were the pranksters.

PERHAPS READERS REMEMBER that the Walker Cup is named for ex-President George Bush's grandfather, George Herbert Walker, who was USGA president in 1920. Prescott S. Bush, the president's father, was USGA president in 1935, and Prescott S. Bush, Jr., was a USGA committeeman during four of the eight years that I served. We became good friends and he was a fun golf partner.

All told, the week in Scotland was truly rewarding, a week the Jemisons remember fondly.

Two years later I was invited to become a member of the Royal and Ancient Golf Club, a signal honor. You don't apply to become an R and A member; you must be invited. I didn't know then and still don't know who my sponsors were; regardless, I was most grateful and continue today to enjoy my membership despite being only an infrequent visitor to St. Andrews.

My membership, which has no connection with the USGA/R and A joint meetings, entitles me to full use of the clubhouse and the privilege to sponsor as guests a visit in the club by a limited number of nonmembers who wish to share the tradition and history.

Incidentally, President Gerald Ford was invited the same year to become a member. Later, because he found he couldn't use the membership he asked to be removed from the roll because he was filling a place someone else might enjoy.

In 1987 when Jess Ann and I returned to Europe to retrace my World War II route, I again played the Old Course at St. Andrews. I now have played all four courses there. I was fortunate enough, at age 66, to score 76 on the Old Course on a misty, windy day, a creditable showing, I think.

All golfers throughout the world should endeavor to visit St. Andrews at least once to experience the tradition and beginnings of the great game of golf.

16
Lucky Me

O ut of the blue one day, Charley Boswell turned to me and said, "Elbo, you ought to be in the Alabama Sports Hall of Fame."

I don't remember what we had been talking about, but because Bos usually measured what he said, I thought he either must have run out of conversation or was getting drowsy.

"Yeah," I mumbled as if he had told me I ought to run for president.

As almost-perennial national blind golf champion, Bos had entered the Alabama sports hall in 1972, Sam Byrd had in 1974 and Selma's Otey Crisman in 1979. That was the crop — three golfers in 13 years.

Champion golfers such as Sam Perry not in his state's Sports Hall of Fame? Perry had been state champion four times and Southern champion three times before losing his life at 36 in World War II. To Alabama golfers generally and to a casual observer like me, that meant golfers weren't getting much notice from the people who made the selections.

I later learned that Sam had not been inducted simply because most people in the state do not understand that a candidate first must be nominated. Because Sam had lost his life in World War II, many people had not heard of him.

So, as I said, Bos's idle remark seemed just that, idle. I would learn later that he had meant what he said. He already had begun to promote my nomination. He had sent out 111 letters asking endorsement of my nomination; 109 responded favorably and the other two just didn't answer, he told me later.

Unbeknownst to me, he had prepared a Jemison biographical sketch and included it with his letter. The capsule included the championships I had won and my service in golf administration, highlighted by my eight years on the USGA Executive Committee during which I spearheaded the Associates (Members) Program with the assistance of President Ford and Arnold Palmer.

When Bos committed to something, he didn't hold back. I presume that's the way it was with my nomination to the hall because when the 1982 inductees list was announced, my name was on it.

I was in august company indeed. Other 1982 inductees were to be ex-

With fellow members of the Alabama Sports Hall of Fame at a recent sports hall banquet.

Jerry Pate was a surprise guest at my induction into the Alabama Sports Hall of Fame. This picture was made just after Jerry had won the 1976 U.S. Open at Atlanta, where I was on officiating duty.
(Associated Press Photo)

major league baseball player Frank Bolling; ex-Alabama football coach Paul Burnum; the late *Birmingham News* sports editor Benny Marshall, and one-time Auburn football stars Tucker Frederickson and Zeke Smith.

A Friday night reception gave inductees opportunity to say hello to and swap experiences with many of the sports stars who had preceded us into the hall. The Saturday night induction ceremony was incredibly rewarding for the six of us, the highlight of my golf career as it probably was the career highlight for my fellow inductees.

I know my family members, Jess Ann and our three children — Anne, Bo and Richard — were genuinely pleased for the old man, forgetting for that evening (I hoped) the many days I was out on the golf course or away at a tournament or an Executive Committee meeting. Their faces reflected their pride, and I felt deep appreciation all over again for their putting up with the demands of my long golf life.

A very special part of that induction weekend was the totally unexpected (to me anyway) appearance of two alltime great golfers, Byron Nelson and Jerry Pate.

To me, Texan Byron Nelson was and is the No. 1 golfer of all time. I am a great admirer of Bobby Jones, Ben Hogan, Arnold Palmer and Jack Nicklaus, and I am aware of their armies of supporters. But Nelson is my choice for No. 1. No other golfer has won 11 straight tournaments or averaged 68.33 strokes per hole as he did in 1945 when golf courses were not as well maintained as today. Fifty-two years underscore just how great those feats were. Also there was no high-tech golf equipment.

Many times as I glanced at Jerry Pate that evening I recalled the 18th hole of the 1976 U.S. Open in Atlanta when he sank his clinching putt and I rushed onto the green to give him a bearhug. I had known Jerry since he was a kid in Anniston and had seen him perform on the 1975 Walker Cup team in Scotland. Now he was on hand for my big scene.

Nelson, who had won 11 straight PGA tournaments in 1945, delighted the large audience with his remarks, one of the first being: he had been told that "the Alabama Sports Hall of Fame wouldn't induct Elbert Jemison if I didn't come." Pate, equally generous with his praise, echoed Nelson's line that he was told he had to be on hand for my induction.

When hall chairman Frank House presented me my plaque and ring, I felt both humility and immense pride. I thought of the many great Alabama athletes who had preceded me into that hall of honor, and especially of the three golfers already there: Boswell, Byrd and Crisman.

That evening I silently resolved to crusade for other Alabama golfers who I felt belonged in the hall; first and long overdue, the great Sam Perry. While I was a director, I couldn't campaign, but now that I'm a director emeritus, I can and do.

For anyone unfamiliar with how people enter the hall: Anyone can nominate anyone, but the process is not simple after that. The board of directors must deem the nominee worthy — by having brought fame or glory to the state by his or her exploits — of being put on the general ballot of nominees, then must be chosen for induction by one of the Hall of Fame's two Selection Committees, one for the Oldtimers category, one for the Modern group.

Many people had worked hard to establish the sports hall, which was created by the Legislature in 1967 and inducted its first class two years later. Several legislators — among them Holt Rast, Tram Sessions, Joe Smith and later Frank House — were instrumental in legislative efforts to establish the hall.

I served on the board of directors for 15 years and for 12 years served as vice chairman. During that period I came to know many great Alabama athletes and sports leaders. Naming them and others who have been pillars of support for the sports hall, one of the finest in America, would be almost endless. I extend them all heartfelt thanks for the friendships and fun times together.

PRIOR TO MY HALL OF FAME induction, I had been accorded other honors related to my golf career. My writer/editor, Wendell Givens, insisted — primarily he said for family members present and future — that I include honors and awards not already mentioned in this account. I agreed, but I will be brief.

— The Elbert S. Jemison, Jr., Birmingham Golf Association Junior Trophy, created in 1965, presented to the BGA's junior golf champion.

At awards banquet in the early 1960s at Birmingham Country Club honoring the amateur and professional golfers of the year. Left to right: Elbert S. Jemison, Jr., Amateur Golfer of the Year; Jackie Maness; Charley Boswell, and Doyle Smith, golf professional at Mountain Brook Club, Professional Golfer of the Year.

— The Alabama Golf Association Mid Amateur Championship Permanent Trophy, created in 1994 and designated the Elbert S. Jemison, Jr., Trophy.

— The Joe H. King Award for outstanding service and contributions to golf and the Alabama Golf Association. Several others, including Joe H. King, were cited for outstanding contributions to golf and numerous associations.

...nong my souvenirs.

— In 1981, a plaque presented by the Southern Golf Association in appreciation for my many years as a director of the association. I was on the board 30 years and president in 1957 and 1958.

— In 1982, the Distinguished Seniors Award from the Alabama Seniors Golf Association for "unusual and outstanding service to the Alabama Seniors Golf Association and to the game of golf."

— Co-recipient with Charley Boswell in 1989 of the University of Alabama at Birmingham's Athletic and Civic Achievement Award.

— In 1995, the Ike Grainger Award from the USGA for 25 years service.

— In 1986, the Mountain Brook Club's designation of its permanent Senior Golf championship trophy the Elbert S. Jemison, Jr., Trophy.

— Granting of an honorary membership in the Grayson Valley Country Club.

— Elected to membership in the Royal and Ancient Golf Club of St. Andrews, Scotland.

17
Unforgettable Charley Boswell

R ainy weather had foiled our plans to play golf that day, so Charley Boswell and I retreated to his den to a mutual second choice: listening to Glenn Miller music. Like so many others of our generation, we played mellow Miller tunes again and again: "Moonlight Serenade," "I'll Be Seeing You," "I'll Be Home for Christmas," "Days of Wine and Roses."

For servicemen a long way from home during World War II, Glenn Miller music had brought us a touch of home. Now Bos and I listened to it at every opportunity.

At some point in our friendship, Charley said he had often wondered what his response would be if he were given the choice of being blind or being deaf. He said finally he would choose blindness.

Are you surprised, as I was at first? The more I saw his total contentment as we listened to music, the less surprised I was. Being deaf would mean not hearing beautiful music, laughter, or familiar voices. The man had a point, a large one.

Bos's music-listening went beyond Glenn Miller. A sister, Mary Anne Givens, used to give him piano tapes by Roger Williams, Ferrante & Teicher, Floyd Cramer, Richard Claderman and others. He treasured vocals by Gordon MacRae, Eddy Arnold, Maureen McGovern and Jack Jones.

With Boswell, Jim Martin (peeking out), Bo Russell and former President Ford prior to a golf exhibition in Birmingham. It should be noted that Martin conceived the idea of the Boswell Celebrity Golf Classic.

Sometimes he listened to best-seller talking books, partly I think for the genuine pleasure of reading, partly so he could join conversation about books, especially sports and mysteries. He kept up with the news by listening to TV or radio and hearing someone — a family member or very often his loyal secretary, Marie Toliver — read the day's major stories.

To Bos, the major news included baseball averages when they were available. People close to him knew to be careful reading him batting averages. Read one wrong and he'd cut in, "That can't be right — he's hitting better than that." A recheck would prove him right.

SOMEONE HAD TOLD ME that Dr. Alston Callahan, the eye specialist, once had posed a "what if" to Charley. The version I heard:

DR. CALLAHAN: "Charley, if we could give you one hour of vision what would you choose to see?"

BOSWELL, after a pause: "I'd want to look at Kitty for 10 minutes. Then I'd look at each of our three children (Kay, Chuck and Steve) 10 minutes each. That leaves 20 minutes to stand on the corner at First Avenue and

20th Street watching all the girls go by and hoping it's a windy day."

He told me a few years ago that he was asked by doctors at the Eye Foundation Hospital that if they could restore his sight, would he agree to that. He said he told them no, that he had become so adjusted to life without vision, the change would be too much for him to deal with. Then a familiar Boswell grin appeared and I guessed correctly he had a foot-note. "Besides, Elbo, if I could suddenly see again, some of the ladies I've always presumed to be attractive might not be."

Charley always told me to keep my speeches short.

Bos was sharp mentally. He didn't look for or want easy answers and while I don't profess to understand all his choices, I know there was a reason in his answers. And perhaps wisdom that you and I don't imme-diately comprehend. There's the old saying about not criticizing the way a man walks unless you've worn his shoes.

People who make excuses because they have failed or just not succeeded should have known Charley Boswell. He believed that anyone who really wants to can succeed.

Did Charley Boswell have his down times? I never knew and I never asked. My guess is, if he did, they were few and far between. He was too much the positive thinker and doer to dwell on negatives.

He was caring and compassionate. If one of my children as much as caught a cold he would ask for an update. I'm told he was solicitous about brothers and sisters and nieces and nephews, and neighbors. He cared and he kept up.

He also was plain-spoken. If we were scheduled to talk on the same program, he would tell me, "Now, Elbo, don't talk too long, OK? Say what you've got to say and sit down and I'll do the same."

Bos was a firm believer that those who had played sports, especially football, were better soldiers in combat for having played. He felt, and I certainly agree, that competitiveness and the will to win are must qualities in sports and very much so in combat when your life is on the line.

But this book is mostly about golf, so . . .

I KNEW ABOUT CHARLEY BOSWELL, the University of Alabama football star in the late 1930s only from a distance. I knew, for example, that he was the best punter the Tide had had in many seasons, but I did not know other particulars.

When Bos was wounded in World War II (November 1944), our infantry units were comparatively close, about 80 miles, I guess. You probably know how it happened: Just before (not during as some accounts say) the Battle of the Bulge, a tank attached to his infantry company had been hit by German shell fire and as he was about to jump off the tank to apparent safety he heard a soldier call for help from inside the tank. Bos helped him get out but before he could jump off, another shell hit the tank and left him badly wounded; blind, he would learn.

During rehabilitation at Valley Forge, Pa., he was encouraged to try his first-ever swing at a golf ball. He hit it solidly and that opened the door to an incredible record in blind golf: 17 national championships and 11 international championships.

AFTER THE WAR, BO RUSSELL and I were colleagues at MassMutual. About 1948, I think it was, Bo asked me to accompany him to Loveman's department store to meet Charley, who was sporting goods manager there. Bo said, "You need to know Charley. I think you can help him."

The visit was the start of a long, rewarding friendship, cemented by common interests. We both had played football (his at the college level, mine at prep). Both had been combat infantry captains, and both loved golf. And I suppose we had somewhat similar personalities: we were "people" people.

Soon we were getting together often, to talk, play golf and get help from pro Sam Byrd. From the outset, Bos was on the same wave length with Byrd because both had played baseball and knew that power starts in the feet and legs.

Once Boswell and I were playing an exhibition with Byrd and Coach Paul "Bear" Bryant at Pine Harbor Club near Pell City. At some point Bryant mumbled, "I wonder why I keep hooking the ball." Charley told him it was because he was dragging his right foot to the rear, which closed his stance.

Bryant asked Bos how he knew that. Charley said he knew it because he heard spikes on the shoe dragging grass! I'm told he also once told Bryant, "Paul, you've got the worst swing I ever heard."

Some years ago, with Bo Russell along as his coach, Charley and I went to Decatur to play an exhibition for the Sight Conservation people. As we prepared to play, Charley said to the committee chairman, "I know your course is not real long, but how wide is it?"

BOS TOLD ME EARLY in our association that he was comfortable with me. "You're never five minutes late, Elbo, you're five minutes early. I like that." That's how he operated, too, whether he was going to work, out to dinner, or to play golf.

At every opportunity we went to the practice tee. He seemed to welcome my suggestions, perhaps because we shared Byrd's tutelage but certainly because Bos was forever looking for ways to improve his game.

I noticed right off that he used too tight a grip, causing tension in his hands. I knew he had a great sense of feel; he played by feel. For example, when he was on a green, he liked to walk to the cup, reach down and feel it. That seemed to tell him exactly where he was and gave him confidence he could direct his ball there.

One day he asked me, "Elbo, how tight should I grip a club?" I touched his hand and gripped his wrist so I could gauge his grip. Then I showed him by feel how tight his grip should be.

I also noticed early on that Bos would move his head when he stroked a ball. I mentioned that to him and he said flatly, "No I don't. I don't do that." He was stubborn about it, so I put my hand close to his head as he got ready to stroke. When his head bumped my hand, I told him, "See, Bos, your head moved." That convinced him and we worked till he overcame it.

Often after we had worked on a problem, he would tell me on the way

163

With golf buddies and good friends Charley Boswell and Bo Russell.

home, "Elbo, I understand what you were telling me out there today, and I feel like I've improved." He was tenacious about improving and willing to practice until he got it right. I thought about his punting at Alabama and how he must have worked on that day after day.

On his occasional bad shots, Bos would look discouraged, but I would tell him, "Don't expect to make every shot just right. Besides, your last shot wasn't all that bad." No matter, he wanted to hit right every time!

WHEN GRANT THOMAS, a longtime Ensley buddy and his second golf coach, died, Bos looked around for another coach.

A cousin, Dick Cox, had been the first coach. After Grant Thomas and not necessarily in order were E.T. Walrond, Sam Jaffe, Bill Mogge, Cecil

Ingram, Jr., Jim Martin, Cary Tuck, and of course, Bo Russell. Three of us — Martin, Ingram and I — were instructors, too. We served gladly without pay.

Bo wasn't an experienced golfer, but he and Charley had become close friends and Bo began filling the gap as interim coach. What he lacked in finesse, Bo more than made up in good nature and willingness. Soon the partnership became permanent.

The late Alf Van Hoose, *Birmingham News* sports editor, often spoke of the potential feature story about the Alabama-Auburn camaraderie in the Boswell-Russell partnership.

Charley, Bo and I went to Las Vegas in 1982 to participate in Gordon MacRae's charity golf event for the National Council on Alcoholism. Gordon had already played in the Charley Boswell Celebrity Golf Classic, which would raise more than a million dollars for the Eye Foundation Hospital.

As was his custom, Charley took along his coffee pot and three mugs. Our first morning in Vegas, he got up early, made coffee and filled a mug to take to Bo, who was several rooms down the hall. An elderly couple saw this big guy in his pajamas and golf cap moving down the hall, touching and counting doors; he knew where Bo's room was. I happened to see what was going on and explained to the astonished couple who Charley was.

Late one evening after a Las Vegas show and after we had had what Bos called "a few shooters" to relax, he and I began singing a spontaneous rendition of "Stars Fell on Alabama." Two young women who identified themselves as booking agents came over and asked who we were. Bos and I grinned and, not feeling any pain, identified ourselves as the "Dixie Humming Birds. We do little jobs in night clubs."

"Sing it again," one of the "agents" said, "and we'll tape it. But you'll have to sign a waiver. Who's your manager?"

"Why he's right here . . . Mr. Russell." Bo went along with that but was about to crack up. We auditioned but never saw the "agents" again and there went our singing careers. The "agents" never noticed that Bos was blind.

Charley had to try the slot machines, of course, and nothing but the silver-dollar bandits would do for him. We were a few machines apart when suddenly I heard all kinds of commotion from his direction. He had hit a hundred-dollar jackpot and the big silvers were pouring out. "Elbo, come here quick and tell me what to do!" he hollered. We scooped them up — and he

In Las Vegas with Betty Ford and Boswell. We were there for a Gordon MacRae golf benefit.

started dropping them back in immediately. Before long they were all gone, but he didn't care — he had hit a big one.

In 1981 Gordon MacRae was in Alabama almost a week, appearing as guest soloist with the Birmingham Symphony and anticipating the Boswell tournament, after which he would perform at the followup dinner. Brookwood Hospital had provided a guest suite for him, and he was to be driven to the Civic Center. But someone dropped a signal and no driver went by for him.

Bos was waiting for him at the Civic Center and pacing the floor when Gordon didn't arrive on time. "Elbo," he said, "it's time to start. See if Meredith will go on first." Dandy Don, the Monday Night Football analyst, was cool as always and soon was crooning Texas songs.

Meanwhile, back at Brookwood, MacRae approached a stranger and said, "Ma'am, I'm Gordon MacRae and I need to get to the Civic Center fast." They set out in her car, but on the way she confessed she didn't know (1) who Gordon MacRae was and (2) where the Civic Center was (she wasn't from

Birmingham). Somehow they made it and an antsy Charley Boswell relaxed.

MacRae played in the Boswell tournament twice and never charged a penny, not even for his airfare.

When I was to be inducted into the Alabama Sports Hall of Fame in 1982, Gordon had promised to attend and sing "Stars Fell on Alabama." But he suffered a stroke and months later died. We had lost a great entertainer, a warm friend and a favorite golf partner.

BOS NEVER STOPPED trying to improve his golf and eventually became proficient enough to average in the mid-90s, usually 94 or 95. If he went over 100 he was disappointed; if he shot 90, he felt great.

If you saw Bos play, you probably noticed that his back swing usually was short. He probably was thinking the longer his backswing, the more room for

Charley and Kitty Boswell, Elbert and Jess Ann Jemison host Gordon MacRae in 1981 when he was guest soloist with the symphony.

mistakes. I know, firsthand and from his coaches, that a lot of things would go through his mind: Am I lined up right? How much should I ease up on a downhill putt? Or hit stronger uphill? Have we got the break figured right?

He gave his coaches, especially *Birmingham News* golf columnist Jim Martin, much credit for his success. Yet he knew that when his coach stepped back after lining him up, it was all up to him.

In later years I helped Charley become reconciled to losing yardage, but he never lost his enthusiasm for playing golf. Nor did he forget his hole-in-one on the 14th at Vestavia Country Club. I saw him just miss two others.

He wanted Coach Bo to be as gung-ho about golf as he was, but sometimes Bo, because he wasn't as wrapped up in the game as Charley, seemed to lag a little. Noting one day at Mountain Brook Club that Bo was moving a little slow, Charley casually put his club down and said, "Elbo, let's you and me and Bo have a foot race."

The man was serious. "One, two, three, go!" he called and took off running over clear ground. In a minute he asked me, "Where's Bo?" He didn't want to lose even an impromptu foot race to Bo. And where was Bo? Yards behind, chuckling and not caring one whit who won.

THROUGH THE YEARS various stories have made the rounds about Bos. One oft-told account had him driving a golf partner — under the partner's careful instructions — from Vestavia Country Club to Homewood and worrying that he (Charley) had forgotten his driver's license.

I laughed about the supposed incident but doubted that it actually occurred, then Jim Martin said yessir, it actually happened.

Charley's sister Mary Anne Givens said that she and their mother looked out one day from their front-porch chairs in Ensley Highlands and saw Charley driving slowly by! He appeared to be alone, but either brother Jack or Bill was ducking low beside him providing steering guidance.

Charley sometimes drove our golf cart when the coast was clear — no trees or ditches. When he did things like that, he felt in control, not dependent on someone to cart him around. Perhaps that's why he declined an offer of a seeing-eye dog and why he used only a cane as he made his way alone on downtown streets. Mary Anne, employed in the Empire Building across 20th Street from Bos's office in the Brown-Marx Building, often watched anxiously as he crossed the street alone. And I once told him, "Bos, you shouldn't cross the street by yourself." He agreed, but I don't know whether he stopped doing it.

Charley seemed, because of his lost vision, to have sharpened hearing, feel, taste and even sense of smell. He told me that when he arrived at a social event, he usually knew ahead of everyone else what food would be served. He didn't tell me, but I think he sometimes sized up people by their tone of voice. Long speeches, even at the Sports Hall of Fame, made him uncomfortable; he would shift his feet and turn his head — as if looking for an exit!

He could be patient and relaxed, but it bugged him, he told me, when someone took hold of his coat sleeve perhaps to detain him and tell him something.

WHAT IF BOS HAD MISSED the ball on that first swing at Valley Forge — would he have tossed the club aside and never played golf? I doubt it. As he made clear in his book, *Now I See*, it was not his nature to give up.

And what if he had not lost his sight and had pursued his dream of playing outfield for the New York Yankees? I'm guessing, of course, but I bet he would have made it! And after baseball, I think he almost certainly would have followed Babe Ruth, Sam Byrd and other major leaguers into pro golf. He had the balance and timing that golf requires. And the determination — man, was he determined!

When I heard that Charley had suffered a severe head injury in a fall at his home, I was numbed. We had been close friends and golf companions for decades. I had thought of him as indestructible, and after the emergency surgery to remove a blood clot on his brain, I thought he would pull through.

Days and then weeks of little or no communication chipped away at his family's hope that he would make it. And even if he did survive, there was the awful possibility that he would be brain-damaged. Finally, Bos began to show signs of reviving. He responded slightly to Kitty's questions. I took his hand and said, "Charley, if you hear me, squeeze my hand." I felt a weak response and all of us took new hope.

Finally one day the familiar grin reappeared and for a time family members could communicate with him. There was hope Bos would live and be whole again. But that was not to be. He developed an infection his body was now too

Boswells and Jemisons hosting Bob and Dolores Hope at dinner at Mountain Brook Club.

weak to ward off and he died Oct. 22, 1995, seven months after his fall.

Charley had said to me during one of our music-and-talk sessions that perhaps it had been his destiny to be blind and to inspire others through his example. He said being blind may have motivated him to more success than he would have achieved had he not lost his sight. I didn't attempt a response: I wasn't sure what I thought about destinies. I knew without question that one of the most inspirational persons I had known had departed. Bob Hope had called Charley "America's greatest inspiration."

Kitty (for whom a medal should be struck) honored three of us — Bos's Alabama football teammate Holt Rast and eye doctor Bob Morris were the others — by asking us to speak at the memorial service.

Holt recalled his and Charley's football days together at the University and their close friendship since. Dr. Morris told of Charley's concern for others' vision and of his efforts for the Helen Keller Foundation. I suggested that our blind friend could "see" better than most people; he had developed his own ways of seeing. I shared some of our fun times and golf experiences, but saying goodbye was difficult.

MEANWHILE, BO'S HEALTH had been slipping and in early 1997 his big, kind heart stopped. Thus, we had to experience another sad farewell to a great athlete and warm friend.

Mary Anne and Wendell Givens were not able to attend Bo's funeral. Some time later they were visiting Charley's grave at Elmwood when Mary Anne called to her husband, "Look, can you believe this?" She pointed to a new tombstone a few feet from Charley's.

Unplanned, Charley and Bo were still close.

Charley Boswell, whose celebrity golf classic raised more than a million dollars for the Eye Foundation Hospital, is remembered there in a special way.

With the touch of a button, a video that recounts Charley's life and his efforts for the hospital and the Helen Keller Foundation may be viewed in the hospital lobby.

Drs. Bob Morris and Doug Witherspoon worked closely with Charley in the Keller foundation project.

18
The Lighter Side

All that happens on a golf course is not hard-down, steady-knucks golf. Coffee merchant John Donovan and I once were playing a friendly but competitive match at Mountain Brook. John was ready to make a tricky downhill putt on a slick green when, on his backstroke, a beagle dashed across the green.

John was upset, really bothered. "Whoever owns that dog ought to be shot!" he growled.

How could I disagree? "You're right," I said, trying to be emphatic but my heart wasn't in it. The dog didn't stop and its owner went unidentified — to John. But from then on, I tried to make certain that Charley, my beagle, couldn't get out of our yard.

MOST SERIOUS GOLFERS know and abide by the rule that limits them to 14 clubs in their bag. But Murphy's Law (if it can happen, it will) collared Huntsville's Bob Lowry, Sr., at a tournament.

Bob shot his customary competitive first round that put him among the leaders, then discovered he was carrying a 15th club. In those days the penalty was two strokes a hole. Bob could multiply; that meant a 36-stroke penalty for the round, which he readily assessed.

What now? When he played the second and third rounds, he didn't bother to remove the extra club. Why did you do a stupid thing like that, friends asked. "I enjoyed playing the second round with the guys in a lower flight, so I left the club in to level the playing field," he said with a grin.

The 108-stroke penalty in a tournament might have made the Guinness book, but as far as I know, no one submitted it. And Lowry had made new friends.

AT A WOMEN'S SOUTHERN TOURNAMENT that I was helping officiate, a golfer walked over to me, having noted my official's ID, and told me she had been "struck at."

Now that may be a little touchy to handle, I thought. One woman golfer throwing a punch at another, perhaps with a club? Wow, how are you going to rule on that, I thought!

So I had to ask, "Did someone swing a club at you?"

"No," she said, laughing now. "A snake struck at me."

I don't believe that's covered in the rulebook. But that wasn't the only time a serpent came in to play. Dr. Jack Clayton, a friend who played at golf and sometimes added his own brand of spice, once spotted a long snake in the rough. He couldn't resist; he picked it up, twirled it around his head and threw it at a mutual friend, Bob Ramsay. Luckily, it was a chicken snake.

While the subject is snakes, I may as well clean out my notebook, as the sportswriters say.

This actually happened in a tournament. A golfer was on his backswing when, out of the corner of his eye he saw a snake nearby. Safety, he decided in a split second, took precedence. Forget for the moment whether he killed the snake, how does an official — which I was for decades — rule on that? I say self-preservation prevails. He killed the snake.

EVEN IN THE DIGNIFIED game of golf, the best-laid plans and all that jazz.

I played often in Anniston and I had a friend who owned a thrift clothing store there. I saw a pair of pants I liked, bought them, and took them to Shreveport, La., where I was qualifying for the Southern Amateur Championship. I was paired with Lew Oehmig and Billy Joe Patton, with a large gallery on hand.

All went well until the ninth green when I bent over to mark my ball and heard those economy pants split. I knew that nearby spectators also heard the split. I looked up, redfaced I'm certain. A sympathetic woman in the gallery spoke up, "I've got a safety pin." I accepted it with thanks, made repairs and went back to golf.

PREPARING FOR A STATE CHAMPIONSHIP at Selma one year, during a practice round I noted that the usual red and yellow stakes had been replaced by orange.

I asked club pro Bob Burns why orange. Probably a little chagrined, he said Bob Phillips had prescribed the color. Phillips was our amateur-golf rules expert, so I found him and inquired where the orange came from. Bob was a stickler about rules, but as I had suspected, he didn't know all the fine points. He reluctantly acknowledged the error and we had the stakes repainted correctly.

Whatever the rules may have been (or not been) about golf attire, Phillips, our longtime AGA secretary-treasurer, flouted them occasionally. If he ever owned golf clothes, I never saw them. Bob would simply remove his tie, play a round, then put it back on.

But lest readers misinterpret here: Bob Phillips was a close friend of mine and of state golf. He loved the game and the people who played it. Did he perhaps pretend a bit? He tried to play well, but usually didn't.

Alabama golf owes a lot to Bob Phillips. He cared about golfers, and golfers cared about him.

SUPERSTITION AND QUIRKY HABITS are as much a part of the golf scene as they are other sports. I never fell for any of that, but I knew or heard of other golfers who did.

Alf Van Hoose, the longtime *Birmingham News* sports editor, played golf with Charley Fell, Jr., and applauded his skills, among them putting. Sometimes, he said, Fell would take out his putter and talk to it, as: "Now little buddy, I need your help. This is a big round coming up and I want you to come through for me."

Edith Quarles, a friend, obviously thought I could play better if I wore the right color. "Wear something blue tomorrow," she would remind me.

If I did play well, I certainly wouldn't credit anything blue I was wearing. I simply don't believe in such ideas. Sure, I never use red tees and play only No. 3 and No. 4 balls. But superstitious? Not me. That's silly.

FOR THE 1972 U.S. OPEN at Pebble Beach in California, I was on hand as an administrator and was called on for unexpected duty. The tournament starter was late getting there and someone volunteered me to be the starter — announce who was going to tee.

I happen to know that football and baseball announcers always take an advance look at players' names and if pronunciation is doubtful, they get help. Good for them; I didn't have time to look over the names of golfers and their hometowns. So I committed murder on unfamiliar California hometowns.

One of the first was LaJolla, which I called exactly what it looked like: LaJolla, with a hard J. There were snickers, and I heard someone whisper: "That's La Hoya." Now I was not so sure on El Cajon, but I pronounced it as I saw it: "El Cajun." Now there was outright laughter — and help, finally.

Gary Player didn't wait for me to announce him. "I'm Gary Smith," he joked, hoping to save me further embarrassment. By then I was beyond help.

While Frank D. "Sandy" Tatum was USGA president, a sportswriter asked Tatum at a U.S. Open, being played on an even tougher than usual course, if the USGA was "trying to crucify the best players in the world."

Sandy's answer was short and to the point. "No, we are just trying to identify who the best players are." Nuff said.

19
A Gathering
of Friends

A s I was leaving President Ford's office after getting his support
for the USGA Associates program, seemingly as an afterthought
he said, "Elbert, I'm planning an annual benefit golf tournament
in Vail and would like you to play in it. Would you?"

Naturally I was pleased to say yes. But at that moment of farewell cour-
tesy, I had no inkling what acceptance of his invitation would bring: two
decades of visits to Vail, Colo., to play golf and mingle with top professionals,
entertainment stars and headliners from other sports. Jess Ann and our children also went to Vail and that made the trips all the more rewarding.

The Jerry Ford Invitational, as it came to be known, began with modest
numbers of guests in 1977 and grew into the most pleasurable golf event of
my life. The competitive golf, the camaraderie, the dining, the entertainment,
the mountain scenery made the four-day gathering very special.

What President and Mrs. Ford sought and received was fellowship with
friends from all walks of life. Various organizations in the Vail community
benefitted from the success of the event, generously provided by supporters.

As I know from two White House visits and from other close-up observation, the Fords are two of the most genuine, unpretentious public figures
this country has known. The former president is the same with the great and

Brent Scowcroft, Paul Runyan and Jemison.

small, whether talking with a country club president or with a man washing his golf cart.

OF THE 20 YEARS of Jerry Ford Invitationals, I missed only four or five, and those because of family priorities.

Golf was the centerpiece at Vail, but there was more, much more. Once established, the basic format never changed. After arrival Sunday, the schedule, in addition to golf, was:

SUNDAY NIGHT: Welcome Party, sometimes at the Ford residence; informal (no neckties), buffet style. Sort of meet, eat, enjoy.

MONDAY NIGHT: Entertainment by Hollywood and Broadway stars at the large amphitheater. Tickets sold to nonparticipants, a welcome event for citizens of Vail.

TUESDAY NIGHT: The Jerry Ford Invitational Finale at the Lodge with buffet food and drink and special music.

Who was there? Mostly people the President had come to know through golf. In two decades, about 250 every year. Some close friends of the Ford family were there for all or most of the 20 gatherings. From memory and refresher glances at guest lists, some of the guests:

Alabama golfers Buddy Gardner, Hubert Green, Jerry Pate and Larry Nelson, and among others: Byron Nelson, Jack Nicklaus, Jim Colbert, Bob Murphy, Tom Purtzer, Dow Finsterwald, Andy Bean and two pros from the Vail area: Steve Satterstrom, director of golf at Vail Golf Club, and Tom Apple, head pro at the nearby Country Club of the Rockies.

Other sports guests included Don Meredith, Yogi Berra, Bobby Knight, Whitey Ford, George Blanda, Craig Morton, Bud Palmer, Roger Penske and

Joe Garagiola.

The gatherings were bipartisan. Among guests were Tip O'Neill, long-time Democratic Speaker of the House; Gen. Brent Scowcroft, Ford military adviser; White House military aide Bob Barrett, who chaired the overall event; Vail Mayor John Dodson and — well, the list could go on and on.

Entertainers (and I repeat, this is but a sampling): Gordon MacRae, Clint Eastwood, Danny Thomas, Bob and Dolores Hope, Wayne Rogers, Foster Brooks, Dinah Shore, Telly Savalas, Sammy Davis, Jr., Charley Pride, Hal Linden, Jackie Gleason and John Denver.

BECAUSE OF MY GOLF BACKGROUND, I was able to assist in the early years of the golf tournament by scheduling play.

Most years the Invitational was played at two courses, the Vail Golf Club and the Country Club of the Rockies with contestants alternating between the two. Talk about scenery! The courses spread out over valleys; Vail was fairly level, Country Club of the Rockies was somewhat rolling. With such knockout scenery, you must constantly remind yourself to focus on golf.

The 1978 Ford Invitational had to be my favorite for an obvious reason: Our four amateurs and pro won the team event. Our pro was Warren Smith, originally from Gadsden, at that time pro in Colorado. My fellow amateurs included Don Meredith and the mayor of Vail.

My contributions to our team victory came on the last two holes at Eagle-Vail golf course. On the par-3 17th I sank a 40-foot putt from the front of the green and on the 18th I holed out a 75-yard wedge shot for an eagle-3. Thus on two holes I picked up three strokes for our team.

After I holed out on 18, Don Meredith came running over, grabbed me in a bearhug and we tumbled to the ground. The onetime Dallas Cowboys quarterback and everybody's favorite announcer on Monday Night Football, wasn't a proficient golfer in our group, but he was loads of fun as he cracked jokes and relaxed teammates.

Meredith, married to Susan Sloss of Mountain Brook, came to Birmingham for a Charley Boswell Celebrity Golf Classic. He borrowed my driver one day, hit well with it and declared, "I've got to have this club." He still has it.

Don visited our home and played the ukulele in a funfest with the Jemison sons. As we drove him to the airport, he commented, "I know we're lost, but are we making good time?" Never a dull moment with that guy.

MEANWHILE, BACK AT VAIL. One year Dick Ford, the President's brother, had an advance copy of tournament pairings, so I asked, "Who am I paired with?" He glanced at his list. "Dina Merrill."

I shouldn't have, but I asked, "Who's that?"

Jess Ann turned her best flabbergast on me. "You don't know who Dina Merrill is?" In a tone that told any listeners that not everybody in the family shared my blank spot. I took pains to find out before we teed off. Dina Merrill was (1) a beautiful actress, (2) wife of Hollywood leading man Cliff Robertson. Oh.

At the first tee someone suggested that each golfer put up $50 for a pool bet. Dina said she didn't have the cash with her, so could she write a check? Of course. I winced at the reminder when she signed it Mrs. Cliff Robertson.

I winced again when she asked as we walked down the first fairway, "Elbert, you know where the nearest restroom is?"

"But . . ." and again perhaps I shouldn't have said it, "we just left the clubhouse."

"I know," she smiled prettily, "but I've been drinking too much fruit juice."

I pointed to a residence near the No. 3 tee and told her that if no one was home, I thought it would be OK for her to go on in. No one was home, so in she went.

Dina Merrill was personable, attractive and fun to play golf with. More than one guest commented on the close resemblances of Dina and Jess Ann.

ONE DAY AT VAIL I was playing golf with President Ford when he wasn't having a very good day. After he flubbed a shot, I tried to comfort him. "Mr. President, I've heard that it's difficult to be a great golfer and a great lover," I offered.

Straightfaced, he responded, "Who says I'm a great lover?"

The former president phoned me in 1996 to say he was scheduled to speak at Samford University and was coming the day before. He wondered if he and the Jemisons could have dinner. Delighted, I responded.

President Ford stayed at the Sheraton Civic Center, so I asked if he would

Posing during a practice round for the Jerry Ford Invitational at Vail with Dr. Al Swanson, Gerald and Dick Ford.

like to see the Alabama Sports Hall of Fame. The onetime University of Michigan center said sure; he told me later he was very impressed with our sports hall.

I was privileged to meet, through brother Dick Ford, many of President Ford's friends from Michigan, including Dr. Al Swanson of Grand Rapids, the orthopedic surgeon who developed the plastic finger to replace deformed bone.

As you would have guessed, the gracious Betty Ford was an integral part of the gatherings at Vail. Each year she hosted a luncheon for wives and made it a point, Jess Ann told me, to speak with every person at the luncheon. In an early year at Vail, Jess Ann and I sat with Mrs. Ford and Alan Greenspan, the financial wizard. I got through the occasion without asking him a foolish question. I think.

What is it like to play golf in the Colorado mountains? An adventure. Because of the thin air, the courses play shorter, so where you'd normally use, say a 5-iron, you use a 6. But because of the thick turf, there's very little roll.

A gallery might number 8,000 over the full course at Vail, half that at the

At Vail with former President Ford, Jack Tuthill (PGA tournament official) and Gordon MacRae at Vail, Colo.

Country Club of the Rockies. Unless someone like Jack Nicklaus was playing, then the gallery would swell.

All the Ford tournaments were memorable, some more than others, as when Gordon MacRae and I played President Ford and Jack Tuthill, PGA tournament director in a practice round. You don't forget company like that.

Nor do you forget being paired with Gen. Brent Scowcroft, who had been President Ford's national security adviser. Instead of golf shoes, Gen. Scowcroft wore rubber-soles and had a high handicap. So what does he do but birdie the first two holes! After that, he came back to earth. Gen. Scowcroft was a delightful person and was of great service to our country.

The last year at Vail the President and I were paired in a practice round against his brother Dick and Al Swanson. The President loved playing golf and was a fierce competitor.

When Jess Ann and I began going to Vail, we took our children. By the end of the two decades we were taking children and grandchildren. The trips were rewarding for all. While I played golf, Jess Ann would take the youngsters fishing, hiking, bicycling, or horseback riding with the snow-capped mountains as backdrop. At night when the temperature dropped we enjoyed the warmth and friendliness of fireplaces.

Finally the Fords told us the last gathering would be in 1996, and after the final putt on the 18th green, the book closed on the Jerry Ford Invitational.

The 20 years of gatherings with friends are etched in our memories.

We had known camaraderie with friendly, fascinating people from all over the United States. One of our youngsters remarked, "These people are just like everybody else." And so they were.

Friendships made at the Jerry Ford Invitational would not be complete without mentioning Berry Craddock of Colorado Springs and Bubba Cronin of Portland, Ore.

Our thanks to grand hosts President and Mrs. Ford. Theirs was "a gathering of friends" we will never forget. And great credit is due Maj. Bob Barrett and his capable staff.

In a farewell message to his guests, the President wrote, ". . . This 'gathering of friends' . . . should take happy note of everyone and everything around them. Participants, volunteers, professionals, celebrities, sponsors and, very importantly, the residents of Vail who have made it happen.

" . . . We have built. We have contributed to making things better for others. We have laughed. We have competed. We have cared about one another . . . Warmest, warmest regards. Jerry and Betty Ford."

CHAPTER NINETEEN • A GATHERING OF FRIENDS

20
Any Questions?

A fter my talks on golf and/or military topics, if time permits I invite audience questions. Presuming that my reading audience might have had questions if given the opportunity, I have assembled some of the most-asked questions I have heard, along with my answers.

QUESTION: Golf at the championship level is not something the average golfer experiences. Tell us how you were able to tee off with hundreds of people watching, some looking right over your shoulder.

ANSWER: Most of my championship-level competition occurred before television golf really caught on, so the galleries at state, sectional and national championships often were large. And as you described, often with people looking over my shoulder. Through playing exhibitions with great professionals and Sam Byrd's tutoring, I learned to cope with playing before large galleries, making them an asset instead of a liability.

Rather than letting the up-close spectators make me nervous, I psyched myself into wanting to do well with a lot of people watching me. I call it confidence born of thorough preparation.

Also, I felt that if people were interested enough to come out to watch our golf, we should provide them with our best efforts.

QUESTION: You mentioned championship-level golf. Describe the levels of golf as you see them.

ANSWER: We're talking amateur golf, the category in which I played all my career. The pros are a different category.

Generally speaking, amateurs at the championship level compete well in state tournaments, may well have won there. They probably did well on a college team and perhaps have won club championships within their state.

Tournament players comprise golf's middle or second level. These players win club championships and charity events in formalized competition. A tournament-level golfer must be good enough to defeat his peers and must practice frequently to stay reasonably proficient. At this level golfers aspire to win championships but not at the highest level.

The first level, what most of us know as weekend golfers, probably includes 95 percent of the men and women who play golf in this country. If that sounds exaggerated, comparing golf and baseball will help make that 95 percent sound more realistic.

What percentage of baseball players are in the major leagues? Only a tiny portion. The second group is comprised of all minor leaguers and perhaps the best semi-pro and amateur players, such as collegians. All the others — millions? — are baseball's weekenders.

Most weekend golfers play the game to get out of the house, to relax, to be with the guys (the same with women golfers).

Most weekenders I've known play because they love the game and all the trimmings. They realize that you don't have to be real good at golf to enjoy the game. I know some weekenders whose swings look just like they did 30 years ago. They still may aspire to one day winning the club championship or making at least the second flight.

God bless weekend golfers. They're the main reason golf is played by people around the world. Confessions being good and all that: I've been sliding back toward weekend golf for many years!

QUESTION: If there are secrets to winning championships, could you share a secret?

ANSWER: Here's one worth remembering. I never felt that I won a major tournament during the tournament itself. When I won, I accomplished it beforehand — in preparation. I worked to get myself "automatic." For example, I worked until my swing became automatic. Once a tournament starts, you can't start changing or correcting your strokes. Naturally you sometimes must make adjustments, as with weather when a wind kicks up.

My tutor, Sam Byrd, told me the same is true in baseball. The New York Yanks (with whom Byrd played) won World Series games in advance with great preparation, he said. Great athletes fine-tune themselves ahead of time; that gets them in a winning frame of mind.

QUESTION: We don't hear much about golf course architecture these days. What do you think of the apparent evolution from ground to air courses?

ANSWER: Today too many courses are calling for too much air golf; that is, there's only one way to get to the green and that's having to fly the ball there. There should be options to bump and run. that's why many Americans like the British courses, which call for chip or bump and run. It's more difficult for less talented golfers to hit the ball in the air, say over bunkers. They need a ground route to the green as an option.

QUESTION: Which type of competition do you prefer, match or stroke?

ANSWER: In my early playing years, match play was in vogue. In match, you play one opponent at a time, not the whole field as in stroke play. In stroke, because you are going against the field, in amateur competition you seldom know how you're faring at any given moment.

So which type competition do I prefer? The fact is, I've won and lost both ways and I really don't prefer one style of competition over the other. I remember my opponents more from match play, and there's more emotion when the two of you are slugging it out one against one.

QUESTION: Do you sometimes get more satisfaction out of defeating some opponents than you do in defeating others?

ANSWER: That's something I've tried to ignore, but I'm human and the answer is yes — once in a while. There's nothing mean or personal about it, and in most cases it has mattered little to me who my opponent was. But I can remember matches when I sensed that my opponent thought he was a better golfer than I was, and that added a little juice to my feelings. I guess I wanted a little more than usual to win to prove him wrong. So I was just a little more focused and a little more alert to any advantage I could gain. Especially if the match was played before hometown fans!

However, sometimes there was another side to that coin. Occasionally I was matched with a person who seemed to have little confidence in his game who seemed convinced I would win. In such cases I confess that, out of sympathy I guess, I seemed to let up. I remember a semifinal opponent in a club tournament whose manner showed plainly that he expected to lose. And he did, 6 and 5, a one-sided score. Knowing he was embarrassed, I turned in a result (2 and 1) that I hoped would help him save face — and a result I hoped would go unnoticed. I wasn't thinking clearly that day.

A few minutes later, Bob Phillips, *Age-Herald* golf writer and Alabama Golf Association official, confronted me. Phillips was a stickler about rules and reminded me I should be the same. He had the posted score corrected and convinced me my sympathy was misplaced.

QUESTION: Have you ever used flattery to get the edge on an opponent?

ANSWER: Yes, even against my brother-in-law, Dr. George Mathews Jr., at a family gathering in Destin. "Great One," I addressed him as usual "nobody in the state should beat you with your swing. You don't need strokes against me."

I kept the flattery going until he agreed to play me even. I did win, and after that I don't think he was convinced he could beat everyone in the state.

HOW MUCH OF A FACTOR in golf is determination? I never think of determination that I don't think of Nofie Nelson of Oneonta.

In the 1969 State Amateur at Selma, Nofie wanted to break 80, no matter where he finished. But he fell short of that goal and that bothered him. So he vowed to stay in Selma and keep playing until he cracked 80. He was serious, he said, and indeed he was. The word we got was that Nofie went home a week later, goal accomplished, after having shot a 79.

QUESTION: Who is responsible for bent-grass greens coming to this area?

ANSWER: When Hall Thompson built Shoal Creek Club, it was his decision to use bent-grass greens. Those greens set a new standard in this area and resulted in new standards of golf course maintenance at other courses. Great credit should go to Hall Thompson for his contributions.

QUESTION: I've often heard it said in sports: He's playing too long. What are your thoughts about playing golf too long?

ANSWER: Fortunately, one can play golf as long as he lives. However, a golfer who has played at a high competitive level at some point has to face the reality that he can't compete indefinitely at that level. When that time arrives, it's best to accept it. But one can continue playing to enjoy the fellowship.

Baseball's Nolan Ryan pitched a long, long time, but nobody thinks he played too long. And I don't believe you'll hear that Arnold Palmer is playing too long, because he is such an asset to golf. He still loves to play and obviously he enjoys the fellowship.

The same philosophy applies to all golfers at all levels: Keep playing as long as you enjoy it!

QUESTION: You've shared a lifetime of experiences playing and administering golf. Is there perhaps one more to leave with us?

ANSWER: Golfers know the game is full of surprises.

All golfers repair or replace their divots, but not normally in hazards or in adjacent woods.

Mason Rudolph once was in woods left of No. 8 at the Masters. As I was on rules duty at that hole, I saw him, after he hit his third shot, repair his divot deep in the woods.

When I was paired with Billy Joe Patton qualifying for the Southern Amateur at the Belle Meade Country Club in Nashville, Billy Joe played a shot out of a shallow hazard. He repaired his divot, the first and only time I've seen a golfer repair a divot in a hazard other than a sand bunker.

Mason and Billy Joe are class acts.

189

QUESTION: Why are there 18 holes on a golf course?

ANSWER: Whether it's true or not, I do not know, but, years ago I heard that a Scotsman wanted to have a drink of scotch on each hole, and he found out that there were 18 drinks in a bottle.

In Closing...

By and large, golfers respect our game. After all, it's an honorable effort characterized by integrity and pure enjoyment.

Let's keep golf affordable and promote course design that is not too long, not too severe. Let's preserve the environment of our courses — plenty of trees, for example.

The heart and soul of golf is the amateur game, which offers the opportunity to know our fellow golfers. Golf is a test of character and of emotion, the only game I know that requires the player himself to disclose an infraction of rules.

Perhaps Grantland Rice, the dean of American sportswriters, had golf principally in mind when he said it's not whether you win or lose, but how you play the game.